AUTHORITY IN PRAYER

PRAYING WITH POWER AND PURPOSE

DUTCH SHEETS

Bestselling Author of *Intercessory Prayer*

BETHANYHOUSE
MINNEAPOLIS, MINNESOTA

Cover design by Lookout Design, Inc.

Published by Bethany House Publishers
11400 Hampshire Avenue South
Bloomington, Minnesota 55438

Bethany House Publishers is a division of
Baker Publishing Group, Grand Rapids, Michigan.

Printed in the United States of America

ISBN 978-0-7642-0406-7 (Paperback)
ISBN 978-0-7642-0172-1 (Hardcover)

The Library of Congress has cataloged the hardcover edition as follows:

Sheets, Dutch.
Authority in prayer : praying with power and purpose / Dutch Sheets.
p. cm.
Summary: "Dutch Sheets shows how believers don't need to walk in weakness and powerlessness but can take hold of God's promises and be the overcomers He intends them to be. For Christians who desire to pray with greater effectiveness and strength"—Provided by publisher.
ISBN 0-7642-0172-7 (hardback : alk. paper)
1. Prayer—Christianity. I. Title.
BV210.3.S53 2006
248.3'2—dc22 2005032602

In keeping with biblical principles of creation stewardship, Baker Publishing Group advocates the responsible use of our natural resources. As a member of the Green Press Initiative, our company uses recycled paper when possible. The text paper of this book is comprised of 30% post-consumer waste.

green press INITIATIVE

"We live in perilous times! The vigilant parent, pastor, or politician is aware that God's purposes in their lives will be challenged over and over again. Praying with authority is a necessary part of your dominion tool kit. More than a manual for effective prayer, Dutch Sheets distills a lifetime of experience and scholarship into the essentials of high-impact prayer. I began using the breakthrough concepts unveiled in this book the same day I read it. My results have been amazing—yours will be, too."

—Harry R. Jackson, Jr.
Senior Pastor, Hope Christian Church
Chairman, High Impact Leadership Coalition

"In this book, Dutch Sheets brings to the surface something that most of us will readily admit, namely that a good bit of the time we pray, we pray like wimps! Long before I came to the end of the book, I decided that I'm not going to pray like a wimp anymore—I'm going to pray like a winner! I'm thankful for this huge upgrade to my prayer life, and I know that you will be just as thrilled when you read *Authority in Prayer.*"

—C. Peter Wagner
Chancellor, Wagner Leadership Institute

"This is a fantastic, funny, and life-changing book on prayer. It is one of Dutch's best. I highly recommend it."

—Che Ahn
Pastor, Harvest Rock Church
Founder and President,
Harvest International Ministry

DUTCH SHEETS is an internationally known conference speaker, pastor, and author. He has written many books, including *Roll Away Your Stone* and his bestseller *Intercessory Prayer.* Dutch is the senior pastor of Freedom Church in Colorado Springs, Colorado. He and his wife, Ceci, their two daughters, and their three dogs make their home at the base of the Rocky Mountains.

CONTENTS

CHAPTER 1
THE QUESTION

A few years ago I was given a double-billed cap with one bill pointing to the left, the other to the right. The words on the front of the cap, "I'm the leader, which way did they go?" are intended to prompt the obvious question, "Who, really, is in charge?" I loved the humor in spite of the not-so-subtle and obviously asinine aspersion it cast on my leadership skills.

That question in one form or another is asked throughout the world millions of times a day. I recall the day our dog, Mercedes—she's a Boxer, so ugly she needed a classy name—tried to assert her dominance over me. She was young, and the two of us were in a season of trying to establish who would rule our house. I was lying on the floor watching a football game, and she, very ceremoniously I might add, sauntered over and sat right on my chest. She then stuck her chest out, head up, and looked disdainfully at me out of the corner of her eye, glancing proudly at everyone else in the room. Easy to interpret: *I'm in charge here; you will submit to me.* (Maybe it was because I was wearing the cap.)

Mercedes is quite large, and at that time she was already full grown. Having her plop down on me was uncomfortable, not to mention humiliating. The guffaws of my wife and daughters didn't help matters much. Of course, girls do stick together. I took authority over the situation immediately, commanding Mercedes to get off of me. As I'm sure you'd assume, she obeyed her master—and within two or three minutes promptly removed herself! I won that power struggle and have been in charge ever since.

But it is not only people and their dogs that struggle with the "Who's in charge?" question. It is at the heart of all conflict on earth. The question was born in the heart of Lucifer when he tried to sit on God's chest in heaven, and it spread to earth when he passed the question on to Adam and Eve in the Garden of Eden. Satan spewed his poisonous deception, and our foreparents also tried to sit on God's chest. We humans have been wearing a double-billed cap ever since, thinking we're in charge, all the while stumbling around, wondering which way to go. It seems that at every level and in every arena of life, power struggles occur:

- MEN AND WOMEN WRESTLE OVER CONTROL OF RELATIONSHIPS.
- PARENTS AND CHILDREN STRUGGLE WITH WHO WILL RULE THE HOUSE.
- SIBLINGS QUARREL OVER TOYS, CLOTHING, TV, AND A HOST OF OTHER ISSUES.
- BUSINESSES CONNIVE TO CORNER VARIOUS CONSUMER AND INVESTMENT MARKETS.
- SPORTS TEAMS VIE FOR FIRST PLACE.
- DEMOCRATS AND REPUBLICANS STRIVE FOR THE DOMINATION OF AMERICA.
- LEADERS OF NATIONS WAR OVER CONTROL OF LANDS, PEOPLE, AND WEALTH.

Everybody wants to be in charge!

Who is ruling your world? I'm not referring to the big one, as in planet earth. At least not yet. I'm talking about the world you live in every day, your *personal* world. I'm speaking of your home, family, job, health, dog—well, okay, maybe not your dog. God doesn't intend that *any* outside force dominate you. He has given you jurisdiction over your life.

God began dealing with me a few years back about governing my world. And He wasn't referring to Washington, D.C. He was talking about the gray matter in my cranium—my thoughts as well as my house, my finances, my health, and so on. In ever-expanding circles He began to teach me about governing the world around me. God did actually want to use me to influence cities, states, and nations, and has since sent me to Washington dozens of times, to all fifty states on an amazing prayer assignment, and on numerous other prayer journeys.

I want to share with you what He has taught me. I'm certainly not implying that I have full understanding of this or any other aspect of truth. In fact, much of my learning has come through paradigm-stretching assignments and frustration-prompted questions. Desperation often births inspiration, like the day at the airport . . .

I was about to break out in hives I was so tense. It was during a prayer tour to all fifty states that Chuck Pierce and I conducted in 2003–2004.[1] I left my home early, as I frequently did, to fly to another state where I would speak and lead large prayer gatherings that evening and the following morning. That day I wasn't flying my normal airline with which I had special "go to the short line, receive preferential treatment, and get your upgrade" status.

As I stood in the long "NO preferential treatment and NO upgrade" line of this other airline, things became more chaotic by the minute. I don't know if the employees were learning a new system, their computers were malfunctioning, or just what was happening. But everything was in total confusion. I wanted to pass out double-billed caps to all the workers and sit on somebody's chest!

I was already running a bit late, and after waiting twenty minutes with the line not moving, I was getting pretty uptight. My stomach was knotting up, and my anxiety level was rapidly increasing.

I wasn't the only one.

People started pushing their way to the front. Others were shouting from where they stood about not wanting to miss their flight, for the workers to hurry up, etc. And, believe it or not, the workers were beginning to become unnerved and belligerent also! I had never seen anything like it. One lady began to shout about not missing her plane and then began pushing others out of the way as she bullied her way toward the counter.

I remembered a story about my friend and Bible teacher John Dawson, who once had a frustrated and obnoxious lady behind him in an airport line. He decided to witness God's love to her by giving her his place in line. I prayed to receive the "John Dawson anointing" but it didn't work. By this time the "Dutch Sheets anointing" was too strong—she wasn't getting my position! (I'm just as Christlike as John, it's just that God has given me a more intense personality.)

My next thought was to beat her up, but I could see the headlines: "Preacher on Way to Prayer Meeting Pummels Lady in Airport." Then I took a closer look and decided I couldn't have whipped her anyway. She was big and mean—looked like someone from the WWE! We all backed out of her way as she marched forward.

By this time I had decided I would miss my flight and Chuck would have to do the meeting alone. Then in great desperation but no real faith, I decided to pray. "Lord, do something to stop this chaos and get me on my flight," I whispered.

As clearly as I have ever heard Him, the Holy Spirit responded, "You know this is all about you, don't you?"

"I didn't do anything," I replied in surprise. "Don't blame me!"

"This is all about Satan trying to hinder your assignment," I heard.

Remembering 1 Thessalonians 2:18: "We wanted to come to you—

I, Paul, more than once—and yet Satan hindered us," I realized the possibility. *All this confusion and anxiety is about me and my assignment?* I thought. *No way.*

Yet I knew I was hearing the Spirit as He said, *Yes, it is.*

"Well, do something about it," I quietly whispered.

But He was trying to teach me something. *No, you do something about it. Move in the authority I have given you and command the demonic hindrances of your assignment to be ineffective. Declare that you have favor and will get to your meeting on time.*

I did as instructed and then heard, "Now, go over to your right, to the end of the counter, and wait." This ticket counter was on the end of a row next to a wide thoroughfare. I stood at the end of the counter which, naturally, ticketing agents didn't even use.

Almost immediately, though, an agent walked over and said kindly, "Can I help you, sir?"

"Yes, I'm on flight number so and so." I handed her my driver's license, she checked my luggage, gave me a boarding pass, and I was off to my gate—where I was immediately upgraded to first-class!

I was pretty pumped. "Whatever you're teaching me, I sure do want to learn it," I told the Lord. "This is nice."

God has given you jurisdiction over your world—under His authority, of course. He wants you, not sin, demonic powers, negative circumstances, or any other outside force to govern it. I realize this was an extraordinary experience, and I, like Paul, have been successfully hindered a few times. Even so, God *doesn't* want the devil or any of his agents ever to sit on our chests.

The question of who's in control is a governmental issue. We often think of government only in its civil sense, but *Webster's* defines *govern* as "to direct and control; to regulate by authority; to influence; to direct; to restrain; to steer or regulate the course of; to exercise authority; to maintain the superiority."[2] *To exercise authority is to govern.* Praying with authority, therefore, is "governmental intercession." So in essence, this is a book about government—not politics, but prayer! Politicians and government officials legislate through man-made laws and rulings. We legislate through spiritual laws, principles, and activities.

One of Scripture's primary themes is governmental authority. The primary biblical struggle is over the questions "Who will rule humankind?" and "Who will rule the world?" We will see as we progress that the answer to the first determines the answer to the second—yes, in many ways the war is about you and me and who we listen to—*we* are going to help answer the question of who is in charge of the earth. In this earthly war over who is going to rule it, you and your double-billed cap are caught right in the middle!

GOD AND THE DEVIL, OPPOSING FORCES OF GOOD AND EVIL, LIFE AND DEATH, TRUTH AND DECEPTION, SEEK TO GOVERN THE EARTH, BEGINNING WITH YOU.

God and the devil, opposing forces of good and evil, life and death, truth and deception, seek to govern the earth, beginning with you. The more you learn to govern your world the way God intends, the more His cause prospers. God and good will ultimately win, of course. We're promised this in Revelation 20:10: "The devil who deceived them was thrown into the lake of fire and brimstone, where the beast and the false prophet are also; and they will be tormented day and night forever and ever." But God wants to enable each of us to win over evil, governing our personal world *in the now*, every day, and in every circumstance. As we learn to do this, He then needs us to join Him in His overall governing of the earth, becoming active participants in His war against evil and His fight for life. What an exciting adventure life can be!

You were actually created with a nature to rule, to govern, to exercise authority. Using *Webster's* definition of governing, you were created "to direct and control; to maintain the superiority," not be lorded over by other people, evil forces, or even unfortunate circumstances. You're an overcomer, a conqueror. Though this God-given propensity lost most of its purity at the fall, becoming infected with pride and selfish ambition (Genesis 3), nonetheless, the desire in humankind to govern its world was placed there by God.

We are descended from a king, Jesus, Creator and Lord over all, so it logically follows that deep in our DNA we have a desire and ability to rule. God speaks of this motivation in Romans 5:17: "If by the transgression of the one [Adam], death reigned through the one, much more those who receive the abundance of grace and of the gift of righteousness will *reign in life* through the One, Jesus Christ."[3]

This word *reign* means to rule as a king or queen.[4] It refers to our royal nature as sons and daughters of the Most High God. The same word is used in 1 Peter 2:9, where we're called a "*royal* priesthood," again referring to our ruling nature. Children of the King are always to rule and reign in the world and overcome in life. To do so, we must learn to pray with authority and govern through intercession.

In the *Pentecostal Evangel*, J. K. Gressett writes about Samuel S. Scull, who settled on a farm in the Arizona desert with his wife and children:

> One night a fierce desert storm struck with rain, hail, and high wind. At daybreak, feeling sick and fearing what he might find, Samuel went to survey their loss.
>
> The hail had beaten the garden and truck patch into the ground; the house was partially unroofed, the henhouse had blown away and dead chickens were scattered about. Destruction

> and devastation were everywhere.
>
> While standing dazed, evaluating the mess and wondering about the future, he heard a stirring in the lumber pile that was the remains of the henhouse. A rooster was climbing up through the debris and he didn't stop climbing until he had mounted the highest board in the pile. That old rooster was dripping wet, and most of his feathers were blown away. But as the sun came over the eastern horizon, he flapped his bony wings and proudly crowed.[5]

Why did this emaciated rooster insist on rising above the debris to crow? Because it was his nature. His DNA was programmed to announce the beginning of a new day. True to his nature, he stuck out his bare chest and declared, "Wake up, world—a new day awaits!"

And so it is with us. Deep in our DNA is the nature of a King. He speaks to us from within our inner nature, and sometimes when we're under mounds of circumstantial rubble, "in all these things we overwhelmingly conquer" (Romans 8:37). We were made to rule!

I must say at this point, however, that I don't want this book to take on an air of religiosity. There are many religious clichés thrown around in the church, especially in charismatic circles, about "ruling and reigning," being "more than conquerors," etc. Though these expressions are biblical, and we *will* use them in this book, for many Christians they are not reality, but wishful thinking. This—words or actions without the power or substance that should accompany them—describes one meaning of *religiosity* (see 2 Timothy 3:5).

Expressions like these are often only heartwarming phrases of religious denial among Christians—stemming from a mentality that spouts slogans and verses about "overcoming," while people are actually being beaten up by circumstances and walked on by the adversary at every turn. For many believers it seems enough to simply be called an overcomer or to think of themselves as one. Christ's abundant life is for them an appealing hope, perhaps even an intent, but not actual. The tragic reality is:

- THEIR MINDS ARE CONTROLLED BY SIN AND COMPROMISING THOUGHTS.
- THEIR MARRIAGES FAIL ALONG WITH THOSE OF THE WORLD AROUND THEM.
- THEIR CHILDREN GROW UP QUESTIONING GOD'S REALITY OR RELEVANCY.
- THEIR BUSINESSES FAIL ALONGSIDE THOSE WHOSE OWNERS DON'T KNOW GOD.
- THEY WALK IN VERY LITTLE TRUE PEACE OR JOY, EXPERIENCING THE SAME STRESSED-OUT LIFESTYLE AS UNBELIEVERS. (NO WONDER MOST UNSAVED AMERICANS SEE NO NEED FOR GOD. WHAT DIFFERENCE WOULD HE MAKE? THEY QUESTION.)
- THEY SPEAK OF PRAYER'S POWER, BUT RARELY PRAY; EVEN LESS FREQUENTLY DO THEY SEE ANSWERS.
- THEY SPEAK OF AN ALL-POWERFUL GOD, WHO IS "IN CHARGE" BUT WHO SEEMS TO BE LOSING CONTROL OF OUR NATION—OUR SCHOOLS, GOVERNMENT, AND CULTURE AS A WHOLE.
- THEY GLIBLY SING, "COME ON, LET'S TAKE THIS CITY . . ." BUT THEY HAVEN'T TAKEN EVEN ONE YET, AT LEAST IN THE U.S.

Yet off we go to our church services, week after week, learning our lingo and getting our denial fix, all the while wondering why the rest of society—and many of our children—think we live in a make-believe world of religion without reality, performance without power. Talk about a double-billed cap!

What's wrong with this picture?!

Something has to change, and it can. Our God *is* all-powerful, and everything He has said of us is true. His promises are indeed "yea, and in him Amen" (2 Corinthians 1:20 KJV). We absolutely can reign in life and be the overcomer He intends us to be, taking charge of our personal world and changing the world around us. We don't have to allow sin, Satan, or life's circumstances to sit on our chest.

YOU HAVE BEEN OFFERED THE GREAT PRIVILEGE OF HELPING TO ANSWER THE "WHO'S IN CHARGE?" QUESTION FOR THE EARTH.

Beginning with your *private* world—your thoughts, body, actions, and ultimately your God-ordained destiny—you can take charge. Authority is yours.

Then because God established and so honors the principle of authority, He will back you as you walk in the government He has delegated to you regarding your *extended* world—your home, family, business, and possessions.

Finally, God's plan is for you to partner with Him on the earth in broader realms of influence and authority—your *universal* world. Jesus, the sovereign King over the earth, wants to rule institutions, cultures, societies, and governments through you and your prayers. He needs you: Your choice matters and your involvement is crucial. You have been offered the great privilege of helping to answer the "Who's in charge?" question for the earth.

I want to help you take off the double-billed cap, answer the question clearly and emphatically . . . and sit on the devil's chest!

CHAPTER 2

The Author

I don't remember her real name, but it doesn't matter because I just called her "Idiot." She was stubborn, stupid, and strong. To this day I can't forgive her. Don't judge me too severely—she was a horse.

I don't have anyone else to blame for this weeklong test of self-control—which you can already tell I passed with flying colors. The delusional idea of renting the horses for that year's elk hunt was mine. Yes, I said renting: I paid $300 for my misguided, romantic decision to relive the Old West on our annual attempt to "feed the family." I had probably just watched *City Slickers* or some great movie about taming the frontier. Anyway, back to Idiot.

"Do you have enough experience with horses to do this?" the man asked when dropping off the animals.

"Sure," I replied confidently. "All I need is for you to show me how to do that fancy little knot with those straps that hold the saddle on. It's been a while." He gave a big smile, showed me how, and was on his way. *What a friendly guy,* I thought.

The next morning we had our early coffee, dressed in our warmest clothes—it was very cold—took thirty minutes to do the fancy saddle-strap-knot, and we were off for the mountaintop. Idiot was nice on the way up.

But everything changed when we returned to the horses after several hours of hunting. With my incredible knowledge of horses, I had known we couldn't shoot from their backs; they weren't used to it and would have reacted violently. So we tied them to some bushes and wandered off. I don't think horses like being tied to bushes for several hours with nothing to eat or drink, because when we came back to ride them down the hill, they were really mad.

Idiot wouldn't stand still so I could load my gear, then she wouldn't stand still while I mounted up. Also, we were on such a steep slope that when standing on the downhill side it was hard to reach up and over her back to tie things on. And she kept moving up close to the bush, keeping it on her uphill side. Oh, she knew what she was doing, all right.

Like I said, Idiot wouldn't be still. To make matters worse, I had already untied her because the reins were so long I couldn't have reached far enough to untie them from her back. Then the real problem became evident. From the downhill side and with my thick hunting clothes hindering my mobility, I couldn't hike my leg high enough to reach the stirrup—I couldn't get on.

And Idiot was ready to go!

I was fighting her, trying to hold her long enough to mount up, when finally my brother, Tim, succeeded in climbing on Idiot's coworker. (For a few minutes we looked like Laurel and Hardy—or rodeo square dancers.) When Tim finally made it, his horse decided she'd had enough and took off for camp.

Idiot was not about to be left behind. So there I was, hanging on to the side of a moving Idiot, trying to climb aboard from the downhill side of Hell Mountain. One hand on the stirrup, the other holding the reins; one foot hopping off the ground, the other reaching for the stirrup.

"Stop your horse!" I yelled. "I can't get mine to stop with yours trotting."

"She won't stop!" Tim yelled back. "You're on your own."

So Idiot and I did the mountainside do-si-do for a couple hundred yards until we finally reached a level-enough grade for me to jump on. It's a good thing I'm as athletic as I am. In fact, if not for my amazing combination of intelligence and athleticism, I don't think I would have survived the ordeal.

When we finally caught up with Tim, he looked at me and said, "What an idiot."

"She sure is," I said.

He mumbled something that sounded like "not the horse." The animals were moving so fast I couldn't hear him, so I just agreed. We never could get them to slow down—they ran all the way down.

It was a humorous sight when we came crashing into camp. Guys started diving out of the way as equipment flew everywhere. "You idiot!" one of them shouted.

"I know!" I yelled back.

Nonetheless, I had the last word where Idiot was concerned. I made her stay in camp the rest of the week—wouldn't let her go hunting with me. Tim did the same with Idiot's sister. Each time we fed and watered them, Tim gave me a disgusted look and said, "Idiot."

"I know," was always my quick response. "She sure is."

He later gave me a T-shirt with the word *Idiot* on the front in big letters. "Why would I want a shirt with that horse's name on it?" I asked him.

He just rolled his eyes.

The "who's in charge?" question centers around the concepts of power and authority. Many people don't know the difference. I do, as I demonstrated with Idiot. She had the power, but I had the authority. She exerted her power for a while, but I used my authority when I made her stay in camp.

Though many dictionaries and lexicons include "power" in their definitions for authority, strictly speaking, authority and power are not the same. Power is the "strength or force" needed to rule; authority is the "right" to do so. They are governmental twins and must operate in tandem; authority without the power to enforce it is meaningless; power exercised without authority—the right to use that power—is usurpation and is morally wrong.

Where God and Satan are concerned, the issue has never been power, including control of the earth. God is all-powerful. When Satan tried to pull off a coup in heaven, there was a flash of lightning and Satan was gone (see Luke 10:18). No battle, no time delay, no sweat or exertion on God's part—just a release of His power and glory. It is always and only a question of authority.

WHERE GOD AND SATAN ARE CONCERNED, THE ISSUE HAS NEVER BEEN POWER; IT IS ALWAYS AND ONLY A QUESTION OF AUTHORITY.

The same is true with us and our struggle against the kingdom of darkness. Satan didn't gain any power at the fall and didn't lose any at the cross. His power or ability didn't change at either event; his authority, or the right to use that power, *did.* In fact, though Christians often state otherwise, Scripture nowhere says that Christ delivered us from or dealt with Satan's power at Calvary. *He dealt with Satan's authority.*

The King James Version uses the

Greek words *dunamis* (power) and *exousia* (authority) interchangeably, which is unfortunate and creates confusion. In Colossians 1:13, for example, it translates *exousia* as *power:* "Who hath delivered us from the power of darkness, and hath translated us into the kingdom of his dear Son." The verse should read that Christ has delivered us from the *authority* of darkness, as most other translations actually do. Likewise, in Matthew 28:18, Jesus didn't say He had been given "all power," as the KJV renders—He already had that. Christ used *exousia:* He was stating that He had taken back the authority for us that Adam had lost.

This is more than a mere technicality. If Jesus stripped Satan of his power, as some teach, then we no longer need to concern ourselves with him—he becomes a nonissue. Or if we Christians have been delivered from Satan's power, as some teach, then he can no longer affect or control us. We would be able to ignore him completely, which is precisely what many Christians do.

If on the other hand, Jesus dealt with Satan's authority—the right to use his power or abilities—then we would need to deal with him as a usurper, a rebel, a thief that has no *right* to steal, kill, and destroy but *will* if not stopped (see John 10:10). If we have been delivered from Satan's authority and given a higher authority in Christ's name, then we must exercise that authority over the devil's works and power. When we do, God's awesome power will back up our authority. Luke 10:19 refers to this—using our *authority* over Satan's *power:* "Behold, I have given you authority *[exousia]* to tread upon serpents and scorpions, and over all the power *[dunamis]* of the enemy, and nothing shall injure you."

My problem with Idiot was her power, not her authority. She was a rebellious horse, using her greater power to resist me. Though I ended up wasting my money, I really did use my authority to pen her up and keep her from harming me or further interrupting my hunt. Likewise, Jesus said we have authority ("keys") to "bind" the forces of hell (see Matthew 16:19). The term is *deo,* and means to "fasten or tie, as with a chain or cord,"[1] just as I did with the horse. The word is also used in legal circles to mean "legally or contractually binding," which obviously conveys the idea of authority. We can pray with authority, binding or tying Satan legally, and God will back us with His power. So again, what will determine victory for us is understanding and exercising authority.

Will Ford tells how the Lord used him and his wife, Michelle, to move in the authority God gave them and see death averted for Michelle's uncle:

> My wife Michelle had an elderly uncle who had been ill and suddenly taken a turn for the worse. The family was called in to meet with the doctor and was informed that her uncle wouldn't live to see the morning. His vital signs were shutting down. He even had the familiar "death rattle" in his voice, and it appeared to everyone that he wasn't going to be with us much longer.
>
> My wife and I were praying at home, and just when we were about to accept what was happening to him due to his age, we both heard the Holy Spirit say her uncle's time on earth was not yet finished. We believed the Lord was instructing us to take authority over the spirit of death, and speak life to her uncle. When the two of us prayed in this manner, we felt the presence of God and His authority released through us in a powerful way. It was the first time we had experienced praying and using a clear word of knowledge from the Holy Spirit.
>
> The next morning, to everyone's surprise, her uncle was very much alive, and totally turning around! Within three days, he was released from the hospital and eventually made a full recovery! You see, his time was not up. When he recovered, he reconciled with family members and was allowed to catch up on time he had missed out on with his daughters. Two years later, he

went home to be with the Lord, but not until closure was brought into these important relationships.

This is using God-given authority to rule or legislate in prayer—here, actually stopping premature death. I know Will and Michelle very well and can attest to their understanding of spiritual authority. God has used them often in governmental intercession, not only in this situation involving their family but also in many extraordinary adventures of intercession.[2]

Before we endeavor to move forward in understanding our personal authority in Christ, however, we must first look at His ultimate authority over the earth as Creator. This is the foundation all of our governmental prayers must be built upon. I was somewhat surprised when I looked up the word *authority* in my older *Webster's* dictionary, a huge ancient one passed down from my dad—so big that I think it doubled as a weapon. At first I couldn't find *authority* in it. Puzzled, I kept looking. Then I saw it, tucked away under the various derivatives and definitions of the word *author.* The root concept behind authority is authorship, not as in writing but as in origination or creation. One has authority over what one authors. A creator determines the purpose of his creation and holds all rights to it.

THE ROOT CONCEPT BEHIND AUTHORITY IS AUTHORSHIP, NOT AS IN WRITING BUT AS IN ORIGINATION OR CREATION. ONE HAS AUTHORITY OVER WHAT ONE AUTHORS.

God, of course, is creative—it is His nature. And how can a creator not create? So the great Creator went to work, and the first two chapters of Genesis describe the results. One verse in particular describes His pleasure over the outcome: "God saw all that He had made, and behold, it was very good" (1:31).

That God is Author and Creator of the earth and all it contains settles the issue of ultimate authority over it. Jesus has always maintained His ownership and authority. (Again, the authority He won back at Calvary was what Adam lost, not His own.) Little wonder that Satan, through theories of macroevolution and other forms of humanist thinking, wants to dispel belief in God as Creator, for if He is the *author* of all creation, then He has *authority* over all creation, including humankind. If He is not the creator, then authority over the earth and all it contains is up for grabs.

Bible-believing Christians know that Jesus is Author and Creator of everything and therefore has authority over all. The following New Testament verses, as well as Genesis 1–2, make clear His claims:

> All things were made and came into existence through Him; and without Him was not even one thing made that has come into being. (John 1:3 AMP)
>
> From Him and through Him and to Him are all things. [For all things originate with Him and come from Him; all things live through Him, and all things center in and tend to consummate and to end in Him.] To Him be glory forever! Amen (so be it). (Romans 11:36 AMP)
>
> By Him all things were created, both in the heavens and on earth, visible and invisible, whether thrones or dominions or rulers or authorities—all things have been created by Him and for Him. And He is before all things, and in Him all things hold together. (Colossians 1:16–17)

Kings, dictators, other forms of human government, organizations, and even individuals may think they own the earth and therefore have complete authority over parts of it. But they do not; they are simply stewards. The earth is the Lord's and all it contains (see Psalm 24:1). Psalm 75:7 says, "God is the Judge; He puts down one and exalts another." Even the authority in which Satan operates is a limited amount conferred upon him by the decisions and actions of human beings. Like ours, in a sense, his has been delegated to him—not by God, but by the actions of people.

As already stated, Satan, through deception and man-centered thinking, has tried to convince the world that there is no Creator and, accordingly, that ownership and authority over the earth really is up for grabs.

- EDUCATORS WHO BUY INTO THIS REASONING BELIEVE THEY HAVE THE RIGHT TO DICTATE GOD'S PLACE AND ROLE IN THE PROCESS OF TEACHING.
- SOME GOVERNMENT OFFICIALS BELIEVE THEY HAVE MORE AUTHORITY THAN GOD OVER THEIR JURISDICTION, AND THAT THEY EVEN POSSESS THE RIGHT TO DICTATE HIS ROLE IN GOVERNMENT. (WHAT AN ASININE THOUGHT. AMERICA'S FOUNDING FATHERS KNEW BETTER AND STATED EMPHATICALLY THAT THEIR AUTHORITY WAS DERIVED FROM GOD.)
- ENTERTAINERS AND ARTISTS OFTEN BELIEVE THEIR GIFTS ARE THEIRS TO USE AS THEY PLEASE.
- MANY INDIVIDUALS BELIEVE THEY HAVE THE RIGHT TO RULE THEIR LIVES INDEPENDENT OF GOD'S AUTHORITY.

The Author—the Alpha and Omega, the Beginning and End—knows He has ultimate authority over all creation. *Every aspect of every form of life on all of planet earth is owned by God, giving Him all rights of ownership.* The choice not to submit to Him, though permitted at this point in time, is rebellion. This is why God reminds us that He is the Judge who one day will hold every person who has ever lived accountable for his or her deeds (Revelation 20:11–15).

Establishing this fact that Christ is Creator and Owner—and, therefore, the ultimate authority—of all is critical if we are to truly pray with authority and legislate through intercession. Why? There are probably more, but I want to mention four reasons, then expound on each:

(1) Only those who have authority can delegate it. If Christ doesn't have complete dominion over the earth, He can't give it to us.
(2) Understanding Christ's ownership and authority over all the earth brings great faith to fulfill our callings and assignments, including, of course, our personal world.
(3) Without Christ's true ownership of and authority over the earth, the final outcome of this battle for earth could be in doubt.
(4) We must submit to Christ's authority before He will delegate His authority to us.

In the next chapter we will look at each of these individually. As we do, you will see that the great Author has written His plan for your life before you were even born. His plans for you are good (Jeremiah 29:11), He wants to relate to you as a loving Father (Romans 8:15), and He desires that you partner with Him in the greatest family enterprise history has ever known.

CHAPTER 3
THE POET

Nikola Tesla is the scientist who invented the method of generating electricity in what we call alternating current. Many people regard him as a greater scientific genius than the better-known Alexander Graham Bell.

Philip Yancey tells an interesting anecdote about Tesla. During storms Tesla would sit on a black mohair couch by a window. When lightning struck, he would applaud—one genius recognizing the work of another.[1]

In chapter 2 we stated the importance of knowing that Christ, by rights of creation and ownership, has all authority over the earth and all it contains. We ended by listing four ways in which this understanding affects our ability to pray with authority. Let's look at these four points.

YOU CAN'T GIVE WHAT YOU DON'T HAVE

First, only those who have authority can delegate it. I know this is a "duh" statement, but sometimes the obvious remains hidden. If Christ doesn't truly possess all authority, then He cannot give you the absolute right to rule your world. That would mean, of course, that at times you can only be a victim. It implies that Satan, other people, or circumstances can have the right to trump your authority, dictating whether or not you'll be an overcomer in any given situation. You might believe, for example:

- SATAN HAS THE RIGHT "TO STEAL, AND KILL, AND DESTROY" YOU AND/OR YOURS (SEE JOHN 10:10).
- YOU CAN NEVER OVERCOME DRUGS, ALCOHOL, OR ANOTHER ADDICTION THAT HAS HELD YOU CAPTIVE.
- YOU HAVE TO ENDURE OR PUT UP WITH NEGATIVE CIRCUMSTANCES OR "BAD LUCK."
- YOU ARE POWERLESS TO DEAL WITH REBELLION IN YOUR CHILDREN.
- YOUR GOD-GIVEN DESTINY IS UP FOR GRABS—THAT OTHER FORCES HAVE THE RIGHT TO STEAL YOURS FROM YOU.

The reality? None of these is true. Neither you nor your family, possessions, or destiny are at the mercy of Satan, circumstances, or the world. The Author wrote the ending to your story, and no one but you has the authority to alter it. This doesn't mean everything that happens to you was planned by God. You may have indeed been victimized through abuse or other misfortune. Pain in one form or another may have entered your life. But God is not behind your misfortune. He didn't author it. He *is* the Author and Perfecter of your faith (Hebrews 12:2) and the Author of your destiny—one that includes overcoming *every* single devastation and making you more than a conqueror in the process (Romans 8:35–39).

However, you must agree with Him. You can change His ending if you like, for the Author authorized *you* to write as well. He gave you and only you the right to rewrite the ending to your story, changing it from His to yours.

That God has authored a secure destiny for you can be seen in one of the New Testament words translated *purpose* (see 2 Timothy 1:9;

Romans 8:28). It comes from the Greek term *prothesis*, which means to set forth the purpose of something in advance. "Exposition" is a good meaning for it, as is *thesis* (a word found in the original term). God wrote His plan—an exposition, a thesis—about you before you were even born. Psalm 139:16 bears this out: "Your eyes saw my substance, being yet unformed. And in Your book they all were written, the days fashioned for me, when as yet there were none of them" (NKJV). You have the right to experience this destiny—the authority to insist on it—but you must understand that He has given you this right.

The following testimony illustrates God's ability to heal us from the wounds of devastating circumstances:

> I went through a period of my life where I wasn't sure exactly where I fit in. My parents were divorced when I was a little girl. No one could fully explain the who, why or when to me. All I knew was I didn't live with Daddy or my sisters anymore. For a long time, people told me it had nothing to do with me. I now know that even though it really had nothing to do with me, it still affected my life a great deal.
>
> I searched and searched for relief from my pain. I searched in the bottle and then I tried drugs. Still I had no relief. Yes, the alcohol and drugs numbed my pain. But when the effects wore off, I still had pain. Then finally on a cold Sunday afternoon in Germany in a small army chapel, I heard the voice of God say, "It's time." I remember looking around thinking someone had whispered in my ear. Then I heard the voice again and I knew in my heart that it was time to give my life to God. That was eleven years ago.
>
> What happened to the pain? I gave it all to Jesus. The Bible says, "Cast all your cares upon him, for he cares for you" (1 Peter 5:7). He took away the deep and festering wounds of my childhood. That little lost girl is no longer; a saved and healed woman emerged out of the ashes. "Weeping may endure for a night, but

joy comes in the morning" (Psalm 30:5). People often ask me why I praise the Lord the way I do. To put it simply: He gave me "beauty for ashes."[2]

What a beautiful story of God's faithfulness. For every evil intent of the destroyer of lives, God has a restorative process already planned. We have the right to receive that plan and take charge of our private world. We need not remain a victim.

Another verse confirms God having written our destiny in advance: "We are His workmanship, created in Christ Jesus for good works, which God *prepared beforehand*, that we should walk in them" (Ephesians 2:10, emphasis added). The works He prepared for you to walk in were planned "beforehand," and they are "good." The word *workmanship* is the Greek *poiēma*, which here means an end product or that which is made. From this same term come the English words *poet* and *poem*: God is the Poet, and you are the poem. Though difficult times may cause you to feel otherwise, the Poet has rhyme and reason for your life. The Author had a plan for you before you took your first breath, and no other being, human or otherwise, has the authority to steal it from you.

Even if you've made some bad decisions that have set you back, or others have done things that seem like they could rob you of your destiny, God already has a plan to remedy the situation and get you back on His course. Our English word *prosthesis* also comes from *prothesis* ("purpose"); a prosthesis is an artificial body part, intended to restore lost usefulness. The Creator has already determined how He will restore every aspect of your purpose that Satan or others have tried to destroy, even using the bad as building blocks. And, unlike our human prostheses, God's are not limited in their perfection or ability. This is what Romans 8:28 is speaking about: "We know that God causes all things to work together for good to those who love God, to those who are called according to His purpose."

If you're a believer in Jesus and understand this truth, you know you're never at the mercy of circumstances, fate, luck, or any negative event. Again, this doesn't mean things won't hurt us in life, and I would never minimize the very real pain you may have experienced. I'm only saying that before life dealt you the destructive blow, God had a plan to heal and restore.

THE AUTHOR HAD A PLAN FOR YOU BEFORE YOU TOOK YOUR FIRST BREATH, AND NO OTHER BEING, HUMAN OR OTHERWISE, HAS THE AUTHORITY TO STEAL IT FROM YOU.

> At the Royal Palace of Tehran, in Iran, you can see one of the most beautiful mosaic works in the world. The ceilings and walls flash like diamonds in multifaceted reflections. Originally, when the palace was designed, the architect specified huge sheets of mirrors on the walls. When the first shipment arrived from Paris, they found to their horror that the mirrors were shattered. The contractor threw them in the trash and brought the sad news to the architect.
>
> Amazingly, the architect ordered all of the broken pieces collected, then smashed them into tiny pieces and glued them to the walls to become a mosaic of silvery, shimmering, mirrored bits of glass.[3]

As a Christian, just like these mirrors, you can't be broken beyond God's creative ability to restore. For you, there is no such thing as irreparable damage. You can rise up in the authority He has given you and say, "No one and nothing is going to rule my life but Jesus. I may have lost a battle, but I will win the war. God sees the end result and has already written about my ultimate victory!"

- GOD TOLD THE ISRAELITES THEY COULD CHOOSE LIFE OR DEATH (DEUTERONOMY 30:19). SO CAN YOU.
- HE TOLD NEW TESTAMENT BELIEVERS THAT WE COULD TRIUMPH THROUGH CHRIST (2 CORINTHIANS 2:14).
- WE ARE PROMISED THAT WE CAN ALWAYS OVERCOME SIN AND THE WORLD AROUND US THROUGH FAITH IN HIM (1 JOHN 5:1–5).
- OUR CREATOR HAS SAID THAT HE CAN MEET OUR EVERY NEED (PHILIPPIANS 4:19).

Don't ever accept defeat again. Yes, there are conditions to each of these promises, but only we have the authority to determine whether or not we will meet those conditions. Therefore, only we have the right to determine whether or not we receive the fulfillment of every promise.

My dear friend Will Ford tells how God delivered him from an injustice. But Will had to use his authority and take charge of his private world.

> Several years ago, I was in a situation where I was being forced to pay $70,000.00 that I didn't owe. I couldn't prove it due to poor record keeping, the details of which would take too long to explain. The other company was pressuring me with threats, knowing I didn't owe the money, and that I couldn't prove otherwise. It was a situation where I had all the responsibility and no authority, or so it seemed.
>
> Depressed and fighting back suicidal thoughts and scenarios the enemy was throwing at me, I forced myself to attend a midweek revival service at a local church in town. I cried myself through praise and fought my way through worship. Having been discouraged and depressed beyond description for months, I sat in the middle of 2,000 people feeling all alone. But when the speaker came forward to speak, something unusual happened.
>
> The evangelist walked to the pulpit but before he spoke, he

peered over the crowd. Suddenly he made eye contact with me in the middle of the audience. He then leaped forward from the platform and began walking briskly toward me, without breaking eye contact. I thought, *Is he coming toward me?*

About that time, a lady sitting in front of me stood and threw up her hands, thinking he was coming to pray for her. I, too, thought he was coming to pray for her. But he politely excused her out of my way and said, "I'm sorry, but not you, Ma'am. You, Sir, step out into the aisle." He laid hands on me and prayed, and I went "out in the spirit" for about 30 or 40 minutes. It was the first time I'd experienced anything like this.

While lying on the ground I felt Christ's love coursing through me in a powerful way. With tears of joy streaming down my face, I asked the Lord why He had the evangelist single me out of the crowd. I'll never forget His response. "William, I'll part a Red Sea to make a way for you, and I'll part a crowd of people to let you know how much I love you."

That night, my nightmare of depression, suicide and despair was broken. The moment I heard Him say this, I knew He was making a way out of "no way" for me. I've never felt that sense of hopelessness or struggled with suicide again.

And with the newfound faith and assurance God had given me regarding this matter, I found that I did have authority over this situation—in prayer! Over the next few weeks and months, I prayed and took authority over this unjust circumstance. What did God do? Eventually, the other company was investigated, audited and exposed for corruption. They later went out of business, and my "debt" was cancelled!

That is governmental prayer. God gave Will the assurance he needed, then Will had to use his faith and pray, exercising his authority. Authority released God's power, which caused the situation to change. This is how we rule our world. God will work on your behalf too as you release what He has given you and take charge of your world.

Belief and Faith Are the Same

A *second* reason we must be absolutely convinced that Christ has all authority is that if we don't, we will experience trouble walking in faith.

I recall the prayer assignment the Lord gave me in January 2000. For three years I had been going in and out of D.C. to pray. Before this visit, however, God began to show me that we, the body of Christ, had made great progress in our prayers for America. "I am now going to begin a new phase of changing the spiritual climate over America," He said to me. It was in this meeting, in fact, that God gave me a powerful new revelation and teaching I called "The Divine Shift."[4]

This time, I was not only praying but also speaking in a conference. Before my session, I again heard the Spirit speak: "I want you to change the atmosphere for Me, over this city and nation. Command it to shift!"

I was somewhat stunned. I remember the intimidation I felt standing to the side, waiting to be introduced. Finally, in my insecurity, I said to the Lord, "I sure hope I don't mess this up."

As clearly as I have ever heard God speak, I heard Him that day. "You would have to try real hard to mess this up. Unless you totally rebel against My leadership and refuse to do what I've instructed you, *I'm going to do this!* You don't have to say or do things perfectly. Just do what I've asked you to and I'll do the rest. I need your voice, not your perfection."

Those were some of the most comforting words I've ever heard. I knew God had full authority to do this, and I knew He was authorizing me to be His instrument. I told those present what God had said, made the decree, and what happened next is impossible to fully grasp if you weren't there. God's power *filled* the room! None of the six-to-seven-hundred present doubted it. *And we could literally feel the atmosphere around us change!* It was one of the most profound experiences of my life.

Did things in D.C. and the nation subsequently change? Absolutely! Not long after, we actually heard a police officer on capitol hill say, "The atmosphere here on the hill has completely changed." A few months later The Call took place—a gathering under Lou Engle of at least four hundred thousand young people on the Washington mall to fast and pray for America, which brought further change. Then George W. Bush was elected president, restoring righteousness—not perfection—to the White House. Everyone with any spiritual discernment knew that things began to shift spiritually over America in 2000.

We must be convinced that Christ has all authority over the earth and can use us to release it through governmental intercession! This will release us into a dimension of prayer that most of us have never dreamed of.

The End Is Certain

A *third* reason we must understand Christ's complete authority over all the earth is that otherwise we might think His opponents could ultimately win the battle for the earth. This is laughable. Humanists won't defeat Him, nor will other religions, anti-God liberals, or any other group. Psalm 2:4 says God laughs mockingly at them. As far as He is concerned, the war has never been about who will win ultimate control of the earth—it's about who will be on the winning side with Him. Revelation 11:15 gives the final outcome: "Then the seventh angel sounded; and there were loud voices in heaven, saying, 'The kingdom of the world has become the kingdom of our Lord and of His Christ; and He will reign forever and ever.'"

Those who walk in this revelation have a victorious mindset and walk in greater authority, rejecting a defeatist mindset that believes we must simply hold on as best we can while everything around us falls apart. To know in advance you're on the winning side breeds confidence, vision, and even energetic action.

Lyle Arakaki shares this insight:

> In Hawaii, because of the time difference with the continental U.S., the NFL Monday Night Football game is played in mid-afternoon, so the local TV station delays its telecast until 6:30 in the evening.
>
> When my favorite team plays, I'm too excited to wait for television, so I'll listen to the game on the radio, which broadcasts it live. Then, because they're my favorite team, I'll watch the game on television, too.
>
> If I know my team has won the game, it influences how I watch it on television. If my team fumbles the ball or throws an interception, it's not a problem. I think, *That's bad, but it's okay. In the end, we'll win!*
>
> "In this world you will have trouble," said Jesus. "But take heart! I have overcome the world" (John 16:33).
>
> *As intercessors, knowing the final outcome makes all the difference.*[5]

Power Comes From Submission

A *fourth* and final reason we must understand Christ's ultimate authority is that we can never take charge of our personal world in a way God can *bless* until we do so under His lordship or authority. Most people, and far too many Christians, believe they can do as they please and still expect God to take care of them. This is a great deception. It's like trying to sit on His chest.

Scripture tells us that if we "consent and obey" we "will eat the best of the land." Listen to this verse in its full context from *The Message*:

THE WAR HAS NEVER BEEN ABOUT WHO WILL WIN ULTIMATE CONTROL OF THE EARTH—IT'S ABOUT WHO WILL BE ON THE WINNING SIDE WITH GOD.

> "I'm sick of your religion, religion, religion, while you go right on sinning. When you put on your next prayer-performance, I'll be looking the other way. No matter how long or loud or often you pray, I'll not be listening. And do you know why? Because you've been tearing people to pieces and your hands are bloody. Go home and wash up. Clean up your act. Sweep your lives clean of your evildoings so I don't have to look at them any longer. Say no to wrong. Learn to do good. Work for justice. Help the down-and-out. Stand up for the homeless. Go to bat for the defenseless.
>
> "Come. Sit down. Let's argue this out." This is God's Message: "If your sins are blood-red, they'll be snow-white. If they're red like crimson, they'll be like wool. If you'll willingly obey, you'll feast like kings. But if you're willful and stubborn, you'll die like dogs." That's right. God says so. (Isaiah 1:14–20)

Strong, isn't it? God makes it pretty clear: Choose to obey Him, walk under His authority, and you'll receive the good and avoid the bad. Author-God loves to bless and doesn't like to condemn. Walk in His ways and "feast like kings."

Your story is waiting to jump from the pages of "God's Destiny Book" to the pages of your heart. Believe in His authority and believe in His plan. He is waiting to move you to higher authority than you ever dreamed possible, enabling you to take charge of situations through authoritative prayer.

Let's take a closer look at what the Author planned for us "in the beginning." This will give us an even firmer foundation for our authority.

CHAPTER 4

The Assignment

We've all heard the cliché "If it ain't broke, don't fix it." But sometimes we don't fix it because we don't know it's broken. In some cases the bar has been lowered for so long that mediocre has become standard and normal has become relative. Take, for example, my life in regard to Mercedes. Normal was one thing before she came into it. It is quite another now. I am often asked if things I've written about her are true. Yes, she TP'd my yard.[1] Yes, I had to chase her around my roof one day.[2] Yes, she sat on my chest. Such things are now normal for me. Normal will never be normal again.

- SHE CRAWLED INTO MY LAP THE OTHER DAY—WAS JEALOUS OF THE LITTLE DOGS AND WANTED SOME COMFORT. "OH, HOW SWEET," MY WIFE, CECI, SAID. SWEET? HARDLY. SHE'S NINETY POUNDS!
- SHE EATS ME OUT OF HOUSE AND HOME. THE OTHER DAY SHE ATE A WHOLE CAKE. SHE HAS EATEN STEAKS, BURGERS, CHIPS, CANDY, AND JUST ABOUT ANYTHING ELSE YOU CAN THINK OF THAT'S BEEN LEFT BELOW FIVE FEET.
- SHE DROOLS. LET ME MAKE MYSELF CLEAR—SHE DROOOOOOOLS!
- SHE GOES TO THE BATHROOM—BIG TIME. I CLEAN IT UP. SHE WATCHES ME . . . AND LAUGHS. NO, I CAN'T PROVE IT, BUT I KNOW SHE DOES.
- AND SHE COSTS ME LOTS OF MONEY. IT STARTED WITH

SURGERY WHEN SHE BROKE HER TOE. YES, SHE BROKE HER TOE. YES, THE VET AMPUTATED IT. YES, I PAID FOR IT. THEN SHE TORE A TENDON IN HER KNEE.

"Dogs don't tear tendons," I said to the vet. "Football players do."

"Oh yes, dogs do," he said.

"I guess it'll take a while to heal?" I said.

"It'll never heal on its own. She needs surgery" was his matter-of-fact reply.

"We'll just have to put her down," I told the family later that night. I seriously thought they were going to hurt me. "Well, maybe I could take a few more meetings, write a few more books," I offered.

She healed up nicely after surgery and has returned to "normal." I'm writing another book.

Like I said, normal is relative. So is restoration. We cannot return to normalcy until we know what it was. We, the body of Christ, speak often of restored authority, but we will never fully understand what Jesus restored to us if we don't know what we lost. Let's go back so you can move forward—*let's go back to the future* to experience what God intended as the norm for us.

God never does anything without purpose or intent. Since He knows the end from the beginning, He never has to ad-lib or figure things out as He moves along. You'll never find Him saying He is trying to "come up with" a plan for us; rather, you find Him saying, "I know the plans that I *have* for you . . . to give you a future and a hope" (Jeremiah 29:11). He starts with purpose—the end result—and backs up to design, which is the way something must be made in order to fulfill His desired purpose.

The prophet Isaiah actually speaks of God declaring "the end from the beginning" (Isaiah 46:10). *End* is the same Hebrew word as *future* in Jeremiah 29:11; at times it is also translated *destiny.* God knows and declares—from the beginning—what the end, future, destiny, or purpose of a person or thing will be. In Isaiah 44 and 45, the Lord declared the name and purpose of a pagan king, Cyrus, one-hundred fifty years before he was even born!

Consistent with this truth, God didn't create the earth and then decide what He might do with it. From its inception He knew its purpose—*us*! We, the human race, are the reason God made the earth. It was created to be our home and domain. The Architect of the universe designed the most incredible home for us, made it, placed us on it, and put us in charge of it.

GOD STARTS WITH PURPOSE—THE END RESULT—AND BACKS UP TO DESIGN, WHICH IS THE WAY SOMETHING MUST BE MADE IN ORDER TO FULFILL HIS DESIRED PURPOSE.

The Creator was so excited about all this that after six days of creation He planned a day of celebration. The word translated *rested* in Genesis 2:2 also means "celebrate" and could be translated as such. Have you ever wondered why God needed to rest? I don't believe He ever grows tired, and on the seventh day I believe He celebrated! He was a proud and elated Father, and He just couldn't help but celebrate this "very good" creation (1:31).

Then came our assignment. God's original intent was that this creation would be governed through humans. That's actually what the Hebrew word and name *Adam* means: "a human being (an individual or the species, mankind)";[3] it "usually refers to mankind in a collective sense."[4] Interestingly, the Hebrew term for dirt or soil is *adamah,* from the same root as Adam. God formed *adam* (humans) out of dust from the *adamah* (ground—see 2:7). We are made from the same material as our home!

So God made *adam*—humankind—and named the first one "Adam." I know, that's like naming your dog, Dog, or your daughter, Daughter. It's not that the Creator wasn't feeling quite as creative when naming the man. He was making the point that this first *adam* was the beginning of an entire race of *adams*. He was the prototype, representing all of us. We would trace our ancestry to him and receive from him our nature and inheritance. *What God intended for Adam He intended for all adams, including authority over the earthly realm.*

This is why Genesis 1:26 says God made "man" (*adam*) in His image and then said "let *them* rule." All *adams*, the entire human race, were given authority over the earth. That's exciting! Look out, Mercedes, here I come! (Okay, I'll let it go—it's just such a big wound.)

Psalm 115:16 confirms God's original intent concerning humankind's dominion mandate: "The heavens are the heavens of the Lord, but the earth He has given to the sons of men [*adam*]." This verse's "given" comes from a Hebrew word that can mean ownership but also means "to give in the sense of an assignment"; it means "to put in charge of."[5] God was saying to us adamites, "I'll take care of the stars, planets, and galaxies; but the earth is yours—you're in charge of it." That is why James Moffat, in his translation of Scripture, renders this portion, "the earth he has assigned to men." God didn't give away ownership of the earth, but He did assign humans the responsibility of governing or stewarding it, starting with our private world and continuing to our extended and universal ones.

Why would He do such a thing? Because He wanted a family, born of His very nature, made in His image and likeness, filled with His own breath, with whom He could share His plans. God was saying, in essence, "I want a family. I'm going to create for them an incredible home—the earth—and put them in charge of it. They will manage it for Me and, of course, for themselves. All that I do down there, I will involve them in it."

What a bold and daring plan! This is unquestionably the story of the Bible: God and humans working together, for better or worse.

- SEE HIM NEGOTIATING WITH A HUMAN OVER WHETHER OR NOT HE'LL JUDGE A CITY (SEE GENESIS 18:16–33).
- SEE HIM WAITING FOR A MAN TO PRAY SO HE COULD SEND RAIN (SEE 1 KINGS 18:41–46).
- SEE HIM TELLING A NATION THEY WILL DETERMINE WHETHER HE CAN BLESS THEM OR WHETHER THEY WILL RECEIVE CURSES INSTEAD (SEE DEUTERONOMY 27–28).
- SEE HIM ANGUISHING BECAUSE HE WANTS TO SPARE A PEOPLE FROM JUDGMENT BUT IS UNABLE TO DO SO BECAUSE HE CAN'T FIND AN INTERCESSOR TO ASK HIM (SEE EZEKIEL 22:30–31; TALK ABOUT HONORING PARTNERSHIP AND DELEGATED AUTHORITY!).
- SEE HIM ASKING A PROPHET TO PROPHESY TO A NATION IN ORDER THAT HE MIGHT RESTORE THEM (SEE EZEKIEL 37:1–14).
- SEE HIM WANTING TO REDEEM THE HUMAN RACE BUT KNOWING THAT DOING SO WHILE HONORING HIS INITIAL DECISION MEANS HE'LL HAVE TO BECOME ONE OF THEM! (SEE JOHN 1:14).

It's obvious from Scripture that God works on the earth *through humans*, not independently of them. For example, this is why, in spite of God's sovereignty, things get so messed up on earth and why at times it takes God a while to bring about the changes He wants. Also, lack of understanding of this truth is why we grow disillusioned at times, wondering why God isn't doing a particular thing He promised to do. The answer often is that He is waiting on us to do something! Understanding God's plan of partnership with us answers so many questions.

For example, I was ministering with Chuck Pierce in D.C. in October 2002, when the two snipers were indiscriminately shooting people. Over a several-week period they shot thirteen, fatally wounding ten. The trauma was overwhelming. It was pitiful to see people run to their cars, pump gas while kneeling, and, generally speaking, living lives filled with terror.

In one of our services, God gave Chuck a prophetic word that if the church would pray diligently for seventeen days, the snipers would be found.

Though many people were already praying, the prayer became more diligent and coordinated. Elements of Christ's body began to pray together and with great diligence as the Lord had instructed. *On the seventeenth day* from the prophecy, the snipers were caught. What an example of God waiting for the church to do our part to see breakthrough in the earth!

Looking at a few more definitions will reinforce God's plan of partnership with humankind. God told Adam in Genesis 2:15 to "keep"[6] the garden. This word is elsewhere translated as *watchman* and means "to guard or protect."[7] Adam, as God's government on earth, was responsible to protect it—no doubt from the serpent, since as yet there was nothing else to protect it from. Adam failed in this, and the serpent gained influence.

As Chuck and I ministered in New Jersey on the Fifty-State Tour, I was led by the Holy Spirit to minister on being watchmen. The Spirit kept saying to me that New Jersey was a "watchman state," called to keep the serpent out of their garden. I referred to their state and the nation as "the garden" and repeatedly said, "You must keep the serpent out of the garden."

The people began to chuckle and nudge one another as I spoke. I became somewhat self-conscious and thought for a moment I had made some sort of blunder. Finally someone shouted, "Do you realize we are called the Garden State?" I had known this, but had completely forgotten, which made it all the more powerful to them.

At this point, Chuck came to the microphone and began to prophesy, much as he did in D.C. As he spoke of their watchman calling, he called the state to twenty-one days of prayer and fasting, with actual prayer meetings taking place from three to six in the morning. (I was glad I live in Colorado!) The Spirit had said that if they would do this, the "vipers" trying to come into their state would be exposed. We knew, of course, that the vipers symbolized the evil plans of Satan.

The New Jersey prayer leaders believed the word was from God and took action, organizing early-morning prayer meetings all across the state for twenty-one days. Many fasted. Imagine the encouragement and confirmation of their calling these intercessors felt when toward the end of the three weeks a plan to smuggle missile launchers into the nation through their port was exposed!

We are God's methods. He governs and protects the earth through us. That is what governmental intercession is all about. The concept of authority or government over the earth could not be clearer than in these two passages:

> Then God said, "Let Us make man in Our image, according to Our likeness; and let them rule over the fish of the sea and over the birds of the sky and over the cattle and over all the earth, and over every creeping thing that creeps on the earth."
>
> And God created man in His own image, in the image of God He created him; male and female He created them.
>
> And God blessed them; and God said to them, "Be fruitful and multiply, and fill the earth, and subdue it; and rule over the fish of the sea and over the birds of the sky, and over every living thing that moves on the earth" (Genesis 1:26–28).

> When I consider Your heavens, the work of Your fingers,

The moon and the stars, which You have ordained;
What is man that You are mindful of him,
And the son of man that that You visit him?
For You have made him a little lower than the angels,
And You have crowned him with glory and honor.
You have made him to have dominion over the works of Your hands;
You have put all things under his feet. (Psalm 8:3–6 NKJV)

GOD'S ULTIMATE INTENTION IS FOR YOU TO RULE YOUR PERSONAL WORLD AND TO PARTNER WITH HIS OTHER KIDS IN RULING THE WORLD AROUND YOU.

These passages use two different Hebrew words for *rule*, both of which convey the ideas of authority and government. *Radah*, used in Genesis, means "to subjugate, to subdue, to cause to rule, to reign or to take possession of."[8] That's what we humans are to do on earth! God's ultimate intention is for you to rule your personal world and to partner with His other kids in ruling the world around you. You are a government official!

The term translated *rule* in Psalm 8:6 is *mashal*, meaning "to govern or manage."[9] This same word is actually translated *govern* in Genesis 1:16 and 1:18, the context being the sun governing the day and the moon the night. The sun and moon do a pretty good job; it's you and me I'm concerned about! How are we doing at governing or taking charge of our world?

In 2001, God sent me, Will Ford, Lou Engle, Jim and Faith Chosa, and a thirty-to-forty-member (fluctuating) team of intercessors on a prayer journey to the nation's Northeast. Our purpose was to experience breakthrough over the region and begin the process of turning it spiritually back to Christ.

We went to all the New England states, many of the nation's original cities and settlements, most of the Ivy League colleges and universities, and dozens of other places. It was grueling, but amazing! God did more than we ever dreamed. I won't share the details now—Will Ford and I do that in *History Makers.*[10] What is relevant here are the Lord's instructions to me when He led us on this journey: "Go and command breakthrough for Me in the Northeast; open the Northeast gate of the nation to Me." (See Psalm 24:7–10.)

Shocked and intimidated, I replied, "Well, Sir, we'll give it our best shot."

I'll never forget His answer to me. When I say He spoke to me, I don't mean I heard His audible voice. It was the Lord's small voice in my heart: "I didn't tell you to give it your best shot. I told you to do it. When I told John [the Baptist] to go prepare the way for My Son, turning the people [see Luke 1:16] back to Me, I didn't ask him to 'give it his best shot.' I told him to do it.

"This isn't about you, your abilities, or how perfectly you pray. It is about obeying Me. There has been enough prayer, fasting, and repentance on the part of My church for Me to do this, and it is time for it to begin. Now, go declare it for Me!"

That is *radah* and *mashal*, managing and governing the earth for God. I was amazed by the simplicity of what the Lord had spoken. I realized more than ever before that it isn't about our strength but His. He simply needed some individuals to understand delegated authority and release His kingdom government on earth. We did just that, and the results were astonishing.

God's assignment to us *adamites* took a nasty turn, however, early in our history. So complete and final was God's decision to give Adam this authority on the earth that Adam had the right to give it away. God didn't give Satan authority on earth—Adam did. When Adam decided to submit to Satan instead of God, much of our forefather's delegated authority was forfeited to Satan, who gained great governmental control over all the earth. Our ability to govern our world was dealt a crippling blow. God acknowledges this authority on several occasions in Scripture. Let's take a closer look at how Satan ended up with such influence and what it means for us.

CHAPTER 5

THE CONTEST

I was a great quarterback in high school—at least that's what Mom always told me. And Mom always told me the truth. According to her, if everyone else had been as good as me, we would never have been defeated. Sure, I threw a few interceptions, but they were from my receivers' mistakes, not mine.

I was a pretty good runner, too. Mom said my brother, Tim, and I were the best on the team. We scored our share of touchdowns—would have made many more if our blockers had been better.

I remember when we played one of our arch rivals, Talawanda (no, I didn't make that up). I had no TD passes that game; my receivers weren't playing well, but we were doing okay anyway. The score was tied, and Talawanda had the ball with time for one more play. I played defense also, and I was covering their speedster superstar. As fate would have it, he caught the winning TD on the final play. *This* wasn't my fault either. One of our guys got in my way and "picked" me off my assignment. Mom confirmed this when I arrived home later. She's pretty sharp.

Though the final outcome in the game of life has never been in question, it has nevertheless presented some changes of possession and shifts in momentum. In Genesis 3, Adam fumbled. He blamed Eve, she blamed the serpent, and all of us humans have been blaming one another ever since. Satan recovered the ball, and headship of the earth saw a change of possession. Demons took the field; all "adamites" went on defense.

God, the adamites' coach and, thankfully, the official crew chief *and* chairman of the rules committee, made an important declaration at this point. To the serpent He said, "I will put enmity between you and the woman, and between your seed and her seed; he shall bruise you on the *head*, and you shall bruise him on the heel" (v. 15, emphasis added).

When God said He would crush Satan's head, He was not referring to his physical head but to his *headship* or authority. The Hebrew word *rosh*—also translated elsewhere in Scripture as *chief, leader, captain,* and *ruler*—can refer to a literal head, but it also means first in rank or authority, in much the same way we use it today in regard to a head of state or the head of a corporation. God was acknowledging what had just occurred—Satan had succeeded in taking earth's headship from Adam. But God was also stating that He already had a plan to take it back. "I will win!" He was declaring.

Jesus acknowledged Satan's earthly authority by calling him "the ruler of this world" (see John 12:31; 14:30; 16:11). *Ruler* is the Greek term *archon* and, like *rosh*, also means "first in rank or order." It even means "to govern" and so is elsewhere translated *prince, chief,* and *magistrate.* Christ was reiterating what was known thousands of years earlier in the garden—Satan was at that time the head over the earth.

Satan, during his temptation of Jesus in the wilderness, boasted of this. The worship-hungry serpent took Him to a mountain and showed Him the world's kingdoms, then stated, "I will give You all this domain and its glory; for it has been handed over to me, and I give it to whomever I wish. Therefore if You worship before me, it shall all be Yours" (Luke 4:6–7).

Satan's reference to his "domain" contains the word *exousia*, which we noted (in chapter 2) as the basic New Testament word for authority. "It has been handed over to me," Satan bragged. It was true; Jesus knew it, and He also knew the devil had been sitting on the chest of the human race ever since the turnover was committed.

But this was also why Jesus came. Though He wouldn't accomplish it Satan's way, Christ came to take over the game and set us free. He came to regain the headship Adam had lost. Listen to His words in Luke 4:18–19: "God's Spirit is on me; he's chosen me to preach the Message of good news to the poor, sent me to announce pardon to prisoners and recovery of sight to the blind, to set the burdened and battered free, to announce, 'This is God's year to act!' " (THE MESSAGE).

And act He did.

There was an instant momentum switch when Jesus tucked away the ball. His crushing of the serpent's head was awesome. It began with His earthly ministry: "He went about doing good, and healing all who were oppressed by the devil" (Acts 10:38).

- HE FORGAVE SINNERS, GIVING THEM A NEW LEASE ON LIFE.
- HE DELIVERED THE DEMONIZED, GIVING THEM FREEDOM FROM CAPTIVITY—EVEN FROM INSANITY. DEMONS CRIED OUT IN TERROR AS THE WARRIOR-CHRIST ENTERED THE SCENE.
- HE HEALED MULTITUDES OF SICK, DISEASED, AND PHYSICALLY CHALLENGED PEOPLE.
- HE EXPOSED FALSE RELIGION FOR WHAT IT IS—GIVING ALL PEOPLE HOPE THAT REAL RELATIONSHIP WITH THE FATHER GOD IS INDEED POSSIBLE.
- HE SPOKE TRUTH WITH SUCH CLARITY AND AUTHORITY THAT EVEN HIS ENEMIES WERE OVERWHELMED BY IT.

Jesus wreaked overarching havoc on the sidelines of hell! The kingdom of darkness began to lose momentum—no play worked, no demon was safe, and no human seemed off-limits from the Lord's loving mercy and redemptive power. Satan remembered being kicked out of heaven by this very being, and no doubt he remembered the Genesis promise about his headship being crushed. Unquestionably, he was terrified.

Hell called a time-out and huddled for a strategy session; Satan tried one last power play at the cross. Just when he thought the scheme had worked and he had put away the game, all hell broke loose—literally! In sudden-death overtime, Jesus crossed the goal line, and Adam's race was redeemed. Christ, a flesh-and-blood *adam*, a full-fledged member of the human race and thus legally qualified to take our place, saved the day for all adamites who would accept His victory.

In *Planet in Rebellion*, George Vandeman writes:

> It was May 21, 1946. The place: Los Alamos. A young and daring scientist was carrying out a necessary experiment in preparation for the atomic test to be conducted in the waters of the South Pacific atoll at Bikini.
>
> He had successfully performed such an experiment many times before. In his effort to determine the amount of U–235 necessary for a chain reaction—scientists call it the critical mass—he would push two hemispheres of uranium together. Then, just as the mass became critical, he would push them apart with his screwdriver, thus instantly stopping the chain reaction.
>
> But that day, just as the material became critical, the screwdriver slipped. The hemispheres of uranium came too close together. Instantly the room was filled with a dazzling bluish haze. Young Louis Slotin, instead of ducking and thereby possibly saving himself, tore the two hemispheres apart with his hands and thus interrupted the chain reaction.
>
> By this instant, self-forgetful daring, he saved the lives of the seven other persons in the room. . . . As he waited for the car that was to take them to the hospital, he said quietly to his companion, "You'll come through all right. But I haven't the faintest

> chance myself." It was only too true. Nine days later he died in agony.
>
> Nineteen centuries ago the Son of the living God walked directly into sin's most concentrated radiation, allowed himself to be touched by its curse, and let it take His life. . . . But by that act He broke the chain reaction. He broke the power of sin.[1]

The difference between Christ and Slotin is that Christ not only took our place in death but He also conquered it. He entered the arena of death, took its keys, and became the forever antidote for its sting. And a fact of utmost importance not generally understood is this: *He became the new human head over the earth.* Authority over earth was now safe in the hands of a human that could never lose it again—the God-man, Jesus. Ephesians 1:22 says all things have been placed in subjection to Him who is the "head over all things." Colossians 2:10 says, "He is the head over all rule and authority."

At this point, remember what this does and doesn't mean. Once more: This act dealt with Satan's authority, not his power. You might consider rereading what we said about this in chapter 2. If you're like me, though, you'd rather not have to flip back and find it, so I'll quote it here.

> Where God and Satan are concerned, the issue has never been power, including over control of the earth. God is all-powerful. When Satan tried to pull off a coup in heaven, there was a flash of lightning and Satan was gone (see Luke 10:18). No battle, no time delay, no sweat or exertion on God's part—just a release of His power and glory. It is always and only a question of authority.
>
> The same is true with us and our struggle against the kingdom of darkness. Satan didn't gain any power at the fall and didn't lose any at the cross. His power or ability didn't change at either event; his authority, or the right to use that power, *did.* In

fact, though Christians often state otherwise, Scripture nowhere says that Christ delivered us from or dealt with Satan's power at Calvary. *He dealt with Satan's authority.*

The King James Version uses the Greek words *dunamis* (power) and *exousia* (authority) interchangeably, which is unfortunate and creates confusion. In Colossians 1:13, for example, it translates *exousia* as *power:* "Who hath delivered us from the power of darkness, and hath translated us into the kingdom of his dear Son." The verse should read that Christ has delivered us from the *authority* of darkness, as most other translations actually do. Likewise, in Matthew 28:18, Jesus didn't say He had been given "all power," as the KJV renders—He already had that. Christ used *exousia:* He was stating that He had taken back the authority for us that Adam had lost.

This is more than a mere technicality. If Jesus stripped Satan of his power, as some teach, then we no longer need to concern ourselves with him—he becomes a nonissue. Or if we Christians have been delivered from Satan's power, as some teach, then he can no longer affect or control us. We would be able to ignore him completely, which is precisely what many Christians do.

If on the other hand, Jesus dealt with Satan's authority—the right to use his power or abilities—then we would need to deal with him as a usurper, a rebel, a thief that has no *right* to steal, kill, and destroy but *will* if not stopped (see John 10:10). If we have been delivered from Satan's authority and given a higher authority in Christ's name, then we must exercise that authority over the devil's works and power. When we do, God's awesome power will back up our authority. Luke 10:19 refers to this—using our *authority* over Satan's *power:* "Behold, I have given you authority *[exousia]* to tread upon serpents and scorpions, and over all the power *[dunamis]* of the enemy, and nothing shall injure you."

My problem with Idiot was her power not her authority. She

was a rebellious horse, using her greater power to resist me. Though I ended up wasting my money, I really did use my authority to pen her up and keep her from harming me or further interrupting my hunt. Likewise, Jesus said we have authority ("keys") to "bind" the forces of hell (see Matthew 16:19). The term is *deo*, and means to "fasten or tie, as with a chain or cord" (Zodhiates, *Hebrew-Greek Key Word Study Bible, NASB*), just as I did with the horse. The word was also used in legal circles to mean "legally or contractually binding," which obviously conveys the idea of authority. We can pray with authority, binding or tying Satan legally, and God will back us with His power. So again, what will determine victory for us is understanding and exercising authority.

Jim and Faith Chosa, Native American prayer leaders from Montana, understand these truths in a way few people do, which is why they could be used in the following example of governmental intercession.

In the early spring of 2004, we received notice of the plans of the Dalai Lama to travel to Toronto, Canada, and release 722 occult Tibetan spirits into the Great Lakes Northern Gate of our country. The Spirit of God raised up a great army to prevent this from happening. He inspired us to gather a team at Sault Ste. Marie, Canada, equip them in the ways of territorial warfare and deliverance, and as one Body begin the process of dismantling the defilements in this gateway. We then bound the local demonic spirits thus negating their ability to invite the 722 demonic spirits into the spiritual landscape of this region.

The result was immediate: the Dalai Lama himself said, "Toronto is a very hard place; I could not accomplish what I planned to do." In other words, he could not release the 722 occult spirits into this very important northern gateway, and had to take them home with him.

That is praying with authority! It pleases our Captain when we take the authority He has won back for us and enforce His victory. We should never waste what His heroic efforts achieved.

THE FATHER'S ORIGINAL PLAN IS NOW REINSTATED—HE IS GOVERNING THE EARTH THROUGH HIS KIDS.

I love Christ's trophy acceptance speech in Matthew 28:16–20, after the cross and the resurrection. The disciples had been told to go "to the mountain which Jesus had designated" (v. 16), and there He made His great declaration of victory: "All authority has been given to Me in heaven *and on earth*" (v. 18, emphasis added). Again, *authority* is *exousia*, the same word translated *domain* at Christ's temptation when Satan used it regarding his authority. Jesus was proclaiming, once and for all, "Satan doesn't have it anymore! I took it back, and *I* have all authority—not only in heaven, but on earth as well."

Here is something that can't be proven, but I sometimes wonder about. Jesus "designated" a mountain upon which He would make this declaration. Remember that Satan took Jesus to a mountain, where he boasted of his authority and tempted Christ with it—could this be the very mountain Satan had taken Him to? Was Jesus doing one more "in your face" to the devil? One thing I know for certain: The contest had been decided; victory had been won.

Though he still fights, Satan's doom is sure, his fate sealed; Adam's lost authority is now safe in the hands of the last Adam (see Romans 5). Now we can pray with true authority, knowing that Christ our Head wants to release His kingdom rule through us. The Father's original plan is now reinstated—He is governing the earth through His kids. Lynnie Walker, an intercessor in Nevada, demonstrated this:

At the beginning of 2004, I was awakened with the urgent thought, "A bomb is about to go off somewhere in the world, and you need to get up and pray that it be averted." I began to question if this was my imagination, and besides, I was too tired to get up. But the message came again, stronger as an "inner audible voice." So I got up, went to the closet and knelt and prayed that the plot would be exposed and that nothing would happen. I continued to pray as the Spirit led me, and then I heard, "It's done. You can go back to bed now."

I got up to go to bed, but then I knelt down and added a quick request. "Lord, it would be really nice to hear about this on the news tomorrow, even though 'a bomb that didn't go off' wouldn't normally make the news." Then I went to bed.

The next morning after I awoke, I told Dennis about what I had heard during the night. He said, "Well, let's turn the TV on and see what's on the news."

We turned CNN on and there was the breaking news: "A large bomb was found on the tracks in Spain." It proceeded to explain that a railway worker had found the bomb. It was rigged and ready to blow, but whoever had the detonator must have gotten scared off somehow! There had been a previous bomb that had exploded some days before, killing hundreds of people. The news of the bomb greatly overshadowed the installation ceremony of the newly elected leaders. Wow! It really did make the news!

I came to a humbling and awesome understanding of God's ways. On earth, He has given authority to mankind. He has chosen to work through His people. He woke me up, and perhaps many others, to release His power in this event. All I had to do was say what He was telling me to say, and He responded! How could it get any easier?

CHAPTER 6

The Ekklesia

When Jesus showed up on the fallen world scene, He left no doubt as to His ownership of it:

- HE ESTABLISHED AUTHORITY OVER THE LAWS OF NATURE, WALKING ON WATER (MATTHEW 14:25).
- HE CONTROLLED THE FORCES OF NATURE, ALTERING WEATHER PATTERNS (MARK 4:39).
- HE TRUMPED THE LAWS OF PHYSICS, MULTIPLYING FOOD, TURNING WATER INTO WINE, TRANSLATING HIS PHYSICAL BODY FROM ONE PLACE TO ANOTHER, AND DESTROYING TREES SIMPLY BY SPEAKING TO THEM (MATTHEW 15:36; JOHN 2:9; 6:21; MARK 11:13–14, 20).
- HE DEMONSTRATED AUTHORITY OVER THE ANIMAL WORLD, USING A FISH TO COLLECT MONEY NEEDED FOR A TAX (MATTHEW 17:27).
- HE HAD DOMINION OVER DISEASE, HEALING MULTITUDES (ACTS 10:38).
- HE EVEN DISPLAYED POWER OVER DEATH, BRINGING DEAD PEOPLE BACK TO LIFE (JOHN 11:43–44).

In a plan so daring, bold, and staggering in its ramifications that no one, including Satan's kingdom and even the angels, could guess what it was, God had become an *adam*—a human being—and thereby qualified himself to redeem humankind and win back their lost authority. As established earlier, ownership of the earth wasn't the issue, nor was Christ's authority—He had never lost His. This issue was authority for the human race, whether or not they would re-inherit their governmental rights to earth.

When the God-man, Jesus, paid our penalty and restored us to God, in the process He won back Adam's lost authority. It is now safe in the hands of a human being who will never lose it again. God's original plan was restored: *There is now a race of humans on the earth filled with God's life and nature, capable of relating to Him as Father and managing this incredible home He made for them.*

If they only realized it!

When we are born again, we are no longer simply humans—*adamites*—we are a new race of supernatural beings called Christians (or "little Christs"). In his first letter to Corinth, Paul chastised the believers for acting like "mere men" (3:3). We are not merely human; we are supernatural daughters and sons of the Most High God, filled with His Spirit and anointed to rule. God has His family back and can now get on with His plan of carrying out the great family enterprise of governing the earth.

On a wall near the main entrance to The Alamo in San Antonio, Texas, is a portrait with the following inscription:

> James Butler Bonham—no picture of him exists. This portrait is of his nephew, Major James Bonham, deceased, who greatly resembled his uncle. It is placed here by the family that people may know the appearance of the man who died for freedom.[1]

No literal picture of Jesus exists either. But He can be seen in the lives of His followers, the church. The big question now centers around whether or not we will take on our role of revealing and partnering with God on the earth. Will we allow God to move us back into His original plan, or do we think we are saved just to get to heaven someday? Let's seek a better understanding of what Jesus meant when He said He would build His church. The church is mentioned for the first time in Matthew 16:18–19:

> I also say to you that you are Peter, and upon this rock I will build My church; and the gates of Hades will not overpower it. I will give you the keys of the kingdom of heaven; and whatever you shall bind on earth shall be bound in heaven, and whatever you shall loose on earth shall be loosed in heaven.

When Jesus used the word *church* (Greek: *ekklesia*), the disciples weren't hindered by our contemporary preconceived ideas as to what it meant. Their paradigm of an *ekklesia* differed greatly from what it has become. To us today it is (1) a worship service; (2) a building used by Christians; (3) a local congregation of Christians; or (4) for those who tend toward a more literal meaning, the people of God, "called out" from the world. The last concept is the most accurate, according to a strict translation, but it still falls far short of communicating what an *ekklesia* was when Christ made His stunning announcement.

To the Greeks in Christ's day an *ekklesia* was an assembly of people set apart to govern the affairs of a state or nation—in essence, a parliament or congress. To the Romans, it was a group of people sent into a conquered region to alter the culture until it became like Rome. Realizing this was the ideal way to control their empire, they infiltrated government, social structure, language, schools, etc., until the people talked, thought, and acted like Romans.

When Jesus said He would build His church, He was without question speaking of a body of people that would legislate spiritually for Him, extending His kingdom government (rule) over the earth. His statement that "the gates of Hades will not overpower it" makes much more sense when we understand this. These "gates" are not physical gates, but rather the governmental plans of hell. Biblical gates were often where judges sat to rule or governing councils met to make decisions, and therefore they often symbolized government (for example, see 2 Samuel 19:8; Proverbs 22:22–23). In Ruth 4:10–11, the Hebrew word for gate is actually translated *court.*

In this first decree about the church, Jesus is saying that the kingdom government (rule, decrees, councils) of hell won't prevail over His kingdom government on earth—the church. He follows this declaration by saying He would give to His *ekklesia* "keys" (Matthew 16:19), which also bring to mind authority. Keys lock or unlock, in order to close or open, doors and gates. Christ's church would have keys (authority) to lock the gates (government) of hell and release the gates (government) of heaven.

What a statement!

In *World Vision* magazine, John Robb writes:

> Seven years ago, a giant tree stood on the banks of the Awash River, in an arid valley about two hours' drive southeast of Addis Ababa, Ethiopia. It had stood there for generations, seemingly eternal.
>
> For years, the people who lived in the surrounding district had suffered through famines. . . . In their suffering, the people looked to the tree for help. Believing a spirit gave it divine powers, they worshipped the towering giant. Adults would kiss the great trunk when they passed by, and they spoke of the tree in hushed, reverential tones. Children said, "This tree saved us."
>
> In 1989, World Vision began a development project there, including an irrigation system. . . . But even as they labored to build the system, the great tree stood like a forbidding sentinel of the old order, presiding over the community, enslaving the people through fear. Spirits needed to be propitiated with animal

> sacrifices and strict observance of taboos.
>
> When World Vision workers saw how the villagers worshipped the tree, they knew it was an idolatrous barrier to the entrance of God's kingdom and transformation of the community.
>
> One morning as the staff prayed together, one of Jesus' promises struck them: "If you have faith, you can say to this tree, 'Be taken up and removed' . . . and it will obey you." In faith, they began to pray that God would bring down the menacing goliath.
>
> Soon the whole community knew the Christians were praying about the tree. Six months later, the tree began to dry up, its leafy foliage disappeared, and finally it collapsed like a stricken giant into the river.
>
> The people of the community were astonished, proclaiming, "Your God has done this! Your God has dried up the tree!" In the days and weeks afterwards, approximately 100 members of the community received Jesus Christ because they saw His power displayed in answer to the Christians' prayers.[2]

That's what I'm talking about! Where have we been in our thinking? How have we missed this truth? The church of Christ is not supposed to be a group of harmless, irrelevant, mind-your-own-business worshipers who gather once a week, tucked away from anything public, just to practice their particular mode of religion. This is, of course, what many unbelievers think is appropriate. I frequently hear statements from the media, political leaders, and others that religious beliefs should be kept "private" or that they "have no place in the public arena," and especially that they "have no place in government."

Nothing could be more unbiblical. The purpose behind this satanically inspired dogma is to keep the church from being the church—the *ekklesia.* The Bible brims with examples of God and godly individuals involved in government and other public arenas, intentionally representing God and His will while doing so. The Scriptures are filled with admonitions to minister and promote Christ outside the walls of the gathering place.

If I were Satan and wanted to stop evangelism, the spread of biblical morality, or the rule of God into the earth, I couldn't think of a better way than convincing Christians NOT to be the *ekklesia*—in other words, leave God in the closet, tucked away in their own private world. My first priority would be to keep the church from truly being the church. *My goal would be to leave God without a government on earth.* Then, even though I had lost my authority, I could still rule.

IF I WERE SATAN AND WANTED TO STOP EVANGELISM, THE SPREAD OF BIBLICAL MORALITY, OR THE RULE OF GOD INTO THE EARTH . . . MY FIRST PRIORITY WOULD BE TO KEEP THE CHURCH FROM TRULY BEING THE CHURCH.

While we certainly are not to spread our faith or God's rule on earth by physical force or domination, as some religions teach, implying that we are not supposed to spread our faith and His rule at all is just as ludicrous. We are to invade our culture, workplace, city, nation, etc., with the might of God's kingdom and spread His life and rule *everywhere.* That is what praying with authority is all about. Jesus told us to "make disciples of all the nations" (Matthew 28:19) and to preach or declare the good news of Him "to all creation" (Mark 16:15). The Acts church turned their world "upside down" (17:6 AMP). They upset status quo everywhere they went—and so should we. If a society or culture remains the same after Christ's church shows up, then the church is not being the church.

Bill Johnson doesn't believe in the church staying in the closet, as you will see from the following report. The ministry that took place on an outreach to Tijuana, Mexico, was so powerful it's almost hard to believe. But I know Bill, and I can assure you of his integrity. The report is somewhat lengthy, but so exciting I couldn't decide what to cut out. Enjoy.

> The team met at 6:00 P.M. on a stage set near the most desperate part of the street, which houses prostitutes, gangs and a rampant drug trade. After a time of prayer together during which the team got completely filled with His presence, the surrounding people were being drawn to the spectacle, as in the book of Acts when people gathered around the people of God to see what was happening in the Spirit. However, the rain that had been threatening to pour all day, started to fall shortly after ministry began. Bobby Brown, one of the Third Year leaders, ran up to the microphone, knowing that if the rain continued, it would take away from what God wanted to accomplish that night. He told the crowd that God was going to stop the rain. As he spoke, and then prayed a quick prayer, the rain stopped, leaving all amazed and wondering how it could have possibly happened! News of the miracle spread and even more people came out of restaurants and shops to see what was happening. People couldn't help but be drawn in. One look at the nationals' faces revealed their desire for His presence and a deep longing for a revelation of His love.
>
> For six hours the team preached, received words of knowledge, led people to the Lord, and saw numerous miracles of healing. It was as if what was happening had a momentum of its own because it was beyond comprehension. The team was co-laboring

with God; the Kingdom was coming and the team was simply a piece of letting the Gospel come to life. There were at least six altar calls, but even between asking people if they wanted to receive Jesus, the team connected with people surrounding the stage. Over one hundred people received Christ into their hearts, including five prostitutes, an immigrant from Iran, and a man whose eye had been gouged out in a fight! Many experienced healing in their bodies. A few of the healings are as follows: a man who had been using crutches walked away with the crutches on his shoulder; an older woman could barely walk due to the arthritis in her wrists, knees and hips, but by the time the team finished praying for her, she could walk freely and quickly without pain! Another woman, sick with the flu, was healed and actually felt the "heat" of the fever leave her. A man got saved and healed in his knee. One girl had a tumor in her throat that completely dissolved. An alleged hit-man fell to his knees and repented of murdering people and trading drugs.

For several hours during the night, one young woman, who was obviously demonized, kept trying to access the stage. Many students prayed for her, but she still seemed to act crazily. Dale, one of the students, asked to pray for her and pleaded the blood of Jesus over her. She responded and became completely calm and secure. Her mentor, a known witch, kept trying to disrupt the event as well, yet when she got close enough to one of the speakers on stage, a leader turned and told her to "Be gone!" She ran away and was not seen again.

Another woman, who had been listening from her fifth-story window across from the stage, cried out for Jesus when one of the leaders pointed her out from the stage, asking her if she wanted to know Him.

> Another miraculous event occurred during this time that mirrors the story of the feeding of the five thousand in Matthew. A section of the team was commissioned to find Bibles for the newly saved. They went into a nearby hotel thinking, *Most hotels have Bibles on their bedside tables.* After finding out that the hotel had none, they were not willing to give up.
>
> "Can you check, please?"
>
> The manager opened up a closet behind the desk and saw 15 Bibles sitting inside. The team passed them out, but came back for more a little while later.
>
> "We really don't have any more Bibles," the same manager repeated.
>
> "Please check in the closet again." He opened the closet and found half a box of Bibles on the floor! They came back a while later, realizing that they still did not have enough.
>
> "I didn't even know we had the other box; I really don't have any more, I'm sure."
>
> One of the team asked, "What's that box on the floor in front of you?"
>
> He looked down, opened the box and found it was completely full of new Bibles!
>
> "I cannot believe this!" he stated excitedly. Altogether the team passed out about 70 Bibles.[3]

I am fully convinced that this should be the norm for Christ's church. We should leave the mark of changed lives everywhere we go. However, since we (1) have not understood what it means to be an *ekklesia*, (2) don't understand our spiritual weapons and the invisible spirit realm where they operate, and (3) know we cannot force Christ and His ways on people, our conclusion often has been to assume that we can make very little difference in our world. The prevailing mindset has been to simply place all hope for change in God's sovereignty—a belief that when He wants and chooses to, He will change a particular problem or situation to be in accord with His will. I don't believe we think through this viewpoint well enough to see its complete ramifications. If this concept of God's sovereignty were true, it would mean that places, cultures, and lives are messed up, that suffering is occurring and that people are going to hell simply because God isn't yet motivated enough to do anything about it. I don't blame most unbelievers for not wanting the God that many Christians preach and teach. I wouldn't want to love and follow a god like that.

We will later address the invisible realm of the spirit and our weapons that impact it. We must begin by realizing that we are God's governing force on the earth and that the government of hell can't stop us when we use the authority Christ has given us, becoming true governmental intercessors.

There is another governmental word—used in Acts 13:36—that pictures our role of being God's government on earth. "David, after he had served the purpose of God in his own generation, fell asleep, and was laid among his fathers, and underwent decay." Here, *purpose* is *boule*, meaning counsel, decree, aim, or intention. Zodhiates says it also means "the assembly of the council. In modern Greek, parliament is called *boule*."[4] Let's place that definition back into the verse: "David . . . served the *parliament* of God in his own generation." David knew that in his role as king, he was representing and serving God's government and thus carried God's authority and was answerable to God. Would that government leaders today understood this!

All of them should recognize that they are to represent God's will and purpose in their position of authority. I can assure you that every single one someday will stand before Him and answer for every action and decision. Neither ignorance nor the "will of the people" will serve as an excuse. All pompous arrogance will disappear before the blazing eyes of the Ancient of Days, the true Judge of the universe, who knows the ones who flaunted their rule in His face and mocked His Word and ways. Their prestigious black robes and "honorable" titles will mean nothing to Him. Psalm 2—in its entirety, but especially verses 10–12—is a sobering and appropriate warning:

> Now therefore, O kings, show discernment; take warning, O judges of the earth. Worship the Lord with reverence, and rejoice with trembling. Do homage to the Son, lest He become angry, and you perish in the way, for His wrath may soon be kindled. How blessed are all who take refuge in Him!

But while the rulers of this world are meant to represent God in the natural realm, we, the *ekklesia*, are the spiritual council or parliament of God on earth. We ascertain what His will is, then see that it is implemented by operating in the spiritual realm through prayer and other spiritual weapons.

The word *served—(huperetes)* in Acts 13:36—is also revealing. Literally "under rower," it was used of the several rowers in a ship's galley. The key to their success was the synergy created by rowing together or simultaneously; to take turns rowing would have accomplished little. David, in his day, led a nation of "under rowers"—notice that he was one also—enabling them to row in sync with God's cadence. That's how all government leaders should serve, and when they do, they produce a righteousness that "exalts a nation" (Proverbs 14:34) and enables its people to "lead a tranquil and quiet life in all godliness and dignity" (1 Timothy 2:2).

Jesus truly is building His church, but it is not what we have thought of as the church—a social club, a building on the corner, or even a teaching center or place of worship. It is a government headquarters, a parliament, discerning and insisting on God's will over the earth. We row together, creating an unstoppable thrust of kingdom life into every sector of society: religion, government, education, the arts, media, business, and family. As the true church continues to arise, heaven gains increasing influence on earth, while hell's influence decreases.

JESUS TRULY IS BUILDING HIS CHURCH: A GOVERNMENT HEADQUARTERS, A PARLIAMENT, DISCERNING AND INSISTING ON GOD'S WILL OVER THE EARTH.

Richard Brink, pastor and state coordinator for the U.S. Strategic Prayer Network in Maine, shares the following story that illustrates this kind of authority:

> In 1997, reports came out of New Brunswick, Canada, that the tenth teenager had just committed suicide at Big Cove, a Micmac First Nation reserve. Over the next five years, our church did various outreaches and prayer projects there. We found that besides unemployment and substance abuse, there was something more sinister behind some of the suicides. A local witch doctor was leading many of the teens into the sweat lodges and teaching them how to talk to the "spirits." The suicides increased soon afterward.
>
> We had the opportunity to share Jesus with this witch doctor and also to go on the reservation and pray against this situation.
>
> When we returned last year, we found that there had been no documented suicides since 1997 and that the government was no longer funding the witch doctor's sweat lodges. God showed His mighty power and love to the wonderful Micmac people.

He did so through the church, His *ekklesia.* That was His plan two thousand years ago, and it is still His plan today!

We have seen that when Jesus spoke of building His *ekklesia,* He said He would give them keys to lock the government (gates) of hell and unlock the kingdom government of heaven. In 2000, God began making this real to me in a very personal way.

On a cross-country flight I happened to notice that my departure time was 2:22. I was then seated in row number 22, and the total travel time was 2 hours and 22 minutes. My first thought was what a strange coincidence! Then the Lord reminded me that He had been speaking to me from Isaiah 22:22 about the upcoming presidential election: "Then I will set the key of the house of David on his shoulder, when he opens no one will shut, when he shuts no one will open." *Would God do something like this to bring me confirmation?* I wondered. I knew that keys symbolize authority and that the shoulder symbolizes government (see Isaiah 9:6).

A couple of days later I received a phone call from Sam Brassfield, a spiritual father in my life. While in prayer, Sam had felt the Lord prompt him to call and give me Isaiah 22:22, emphasizing the phrase the key of the house of David. He said, "Dutch, God is giving you a key of governmental authority in this nation."

Soon afterward I went to D.C. on a ministry trip, and there a trusted intercessor friend gave me a gift after the meeting. She said the Lord had impressed on her months earlier to buy it for me, with the instruction that He would let her know when to give it to me. It was a beautiful silver key; her words to me were "This is the key to the city!" I knew it represented the key spoken of in Isaiah 22:22.

Another man, knowing nothing about this, came to me after that meeting with three keys and said, "This morning I felt impressed to bring you these three keys." He too realized they symbolized spiritual authority. Again, I knew they pictured Isaiah 22:22. Matthew 16:19 came to mind, "I will give you the keys of the kingdom of heaven; and whatever you shall bind on earth shall be bound in heaven, and whatever you shall loose on earth shall be loosed in heaven." This had never happened to me before—no one had ever given me keys to symbolize anything.

A week later I was in San Diego with Chuck Pierce, who told me that God had led him to give me a key. He had been given this key in New York by people who said it represented a revival anointing for America. Chuck said, "The Lord impressed me to give it to you."

After that service, another man gave me three more keys, saying he had been impressed by the Lord to do so. Incredibly, the number "222," and no other number, was on each of these keys!

A couple of weeks later I was in California again to meet and pray with my friend Lou Engle. Lou said, "God has been speaking to me about Isaiah 22:22. I've even had dreams about the number 22 and this verse. And at a meeting I did recently, the number of my hotel room was 222."

I came home from that meeting, shared this with our church, and a young man in our congregation said to me, "Just today God directed me to Isaiah 22:22. I felt it was a verse for our church."

Another lady in the service had been awakened from a dream at 2:22 a.m., and she shared her experience with me.

Still another lady in the service, a visiting pastor's wife from New England, had also had a dream the previous night. In her dream there was a man with an old set of keys. She asked him, "What are you doing with those?" He replied that he was going to throw them away because they were just old keys. In the dream she said to the man, "Please don't throw them away. They are precious. May I have them?" He then gave her the keys.

Over the course of two weeks, I had no fewer than twenty-five remarkable confirmations that God was speaking to me about keys of authority and relating this to Isaiah 22:22. He was clearly saying, "I am giving you authority—keys—to impact the nation."

Though the occurrences were happening to me, I realized the message was for the entire body of Christ. We truly have been given keys of authority from God to legislate from the heavenlies (in the realm of the spirit), opening doors that can't be closed by Satan or any person, and closing doors through which evil and destruction might otherwise enter.[5]

I began to trumpet this message around the nation, calling people to pray as never before for the upcoming presidential election. Others, in their own way, did as well. And probably like no other time in America's history, God's *ekklesia*—the governmental intercessors and saints of the Lord Jesus Christ—prayed for a presidential election with such fervency and diligence that it turned the tide. God's will was done, and again, righteousness (not perfection) was restored to the White House.

I have used Isaiah 22:22 many times as a source of inspiration and authority as I have prayed. It has become a life verse for me. Though it is often impossible to measure immediately the effectiveness of intercession, since the fruit often takes time to materialize, consider the following confirmation God gave to assure me of the reality of this verse. . . .

CHAPTER 7

The Dynasty

Then I will set the key of the house of David on his shoulder, when he opens no one will shut, when he shuts no one will open. (Isaiah 22:22)

Go to the White House and, using Isaiah 22:22, close the door to the counsel currently coming to the president that is not My will. Then open the door for My counsel to come to him."

These were the words I heard the Lord speak to me in January 2003. I was in D.C. for a prayer gathering, and on this particular morning we were scheduled to tour the State Department. The actual purpose of the tour was to pray for the State Department as we walked through the building. When I awoke, however, I had the clear impression, *Don't go to the State Department; go to the White House instead,* followed by the above instructions.

I prayed about this for a few minutes and also called Ceci, looking for confirmation. She, too, felt this new assignment was from the Lord, and I determined to obey the prompting. The rest of the group headed for the State Department, while I hailed a taxi and left for the White House.

It was a cold and windy day, and I would be praying outside. Not a good day to forget my overcoat! The more I prayed, the colder I got, which was affecting my attitude. In addition, lots of people were milling around taking pictures, and a group of protestors was shouting one-liners and singing antiwar songs. On top of that, security was strong—I felt that every move I made as I paced in front of the fence was being scrutinized. This made me very nervous, which I'm sure caused me to look suspicious. As I prayed quietly, I was almost sure the entire Secret Service was watching this strange man—me—pacing and obviously alone but speaking to someone. I could imagine that they pictured a hidden microphone or walkie-talkie that enabled me to communicate with someone waiting to detonate a bomb or commit some other act of terrorism.

Suffice it to say that after about half an hour of this, I'd had enough. I felt nothing but cold and frustration—no anointing, feeling of peace, or any other confirmation in my heart that I was accomplishing anything. My self-conversation went something like this: *Sheets, who do you think you are? You're not accomplishing a thing. God gives you a verse a couple of years ago, uses it in your life, and you then think you can do anything you want with it. You're moving in presumption, not obedience. You should be over at the State Department with the rest of the team. You might as well go back to your room and get out of this bitter cold.*

As I turned to go, tail tucked between my legs, a young woman with a baby stroller next to her approached me from behind. When I turned around, she was so close I almost ran into her.

"Excuse me, sir," she said. My first thought was that she was going to ask me for money—D.C. has many panhandlers. But was I ever wrong!

"I hope you don't think I'm weird," she went on, "but is your name something like Dutch Pierce?"

After getting over my initial shock, I had to deal with the incredible offense of being confused with Chuck Pierce! (Actually, Chuck is a close friend, and we frequently minister together.) That this lady wasn't even sure of who I am made what was about to happen much more believable and impactful.

"My name is Dutch Sheets," I said, "and I minister some with a guy named Chuck Pierce. Do I know you?"

"Oh, yeah, that's right—Dutch Sheets. No, you don't know me. I hope you don't think I'm weird," she repeated, "but I heard you speak a couple of years ago, and you talked about a verse in Isaiah—2:22 or 22:2—something like that."

She was getting my attention!

"It was 22:22," I said.

"Yeah, that's right—22:22, the verse about keys to open and close doors. Well, this morning the Lord awakened me early, reminded me of that verse and your message, told me to go to the White House, and said, 'I'll show you what to do when you get there.'"

"I've never done anything like this," she said, "and I don't come here regularly to pray. But the impression was so strong that I bundled up my baby and came to see what would happen. I have really struggled with what I'm doing. It's cold, my baby is probably cold [her baby was well bundled and covered; I've since learned who she is, and I'm sure she's a wonderful mother], and I've been questioning if I really heard the Lord. Then I saw you and thought, *Is that the man who preached about this verse in Isaiah?* I've been watching you for the last thirty minutes, asking God if I'm supposed to approach you, and if so, wondering what to say. I even called my husband, asking him if I should speak to you. He told me that I must! So here I am.

"I know you already know this, and I feel really strange telling you, but the only thing coming to me is that the Lord wants to remind you of that verse in Isaiah and tell you, 'you really do have the keys to open and close doors in the Spirit.'"

I was blown away! And deeply embarrassed.

"Ma'am," I replied, "I've been praying and decreeing some things, using that verse, for the last thirty minutes—in complete unbelief. You have fulfilled your assignment. Now get your baby home where it is warm. I'm going to go back and complete my assignment, this time in faith."

I did. Later, I signaled a taxi and headed toward my hotel. On the way, I got one of the hardest spankings from the Lord I've ever received. It went something like this: "Don't you ever make Me get mama and her baby out of bed again and send them into the cold to teach you 'Faith and Obedience 101,' especially after I've already given you so many confirmations relating to the situation."

Ouch!

This authority for the church to use our spiritual keys, opening and closing spiritual doors, is an aspect of prayer I sometimes refer to as *kingly intercession.* My understanding of this facet of prayer, which I also call governmental intercession, began with an unusual comment made to me by a prophet in the late 1980s and culminated with a statement the Lord made to me in 2002. That's right—it took about fifteen years for me to fully grasp it. Talk about slow! I'm so embarrassed writing this that I've now put my double-billed cap back on. . . .

I knew the prophet's remark was Spirit-inspired, and I asked him what it meant. He said he didn't know. Prophets can be strange like that, saying things they don't even understand. Some of them are downright weird. Those in the Bible were often different than the average person—a camel-haired wardrobe here (John the Baptist), fed by ravens there (Elijah). But perhaps the strangest thing about them, at least to us today, is that they claim to hear from and speak for God!

What a bizarre thought: God might speak and a human being made in His image might be able to hear it.

I'm being facetious, of course. I do believe God speaks today, and true prophets are not weird. But many people don't believe the Lord speaks verbally to us today. Beyond unbelievers, even some theologians and denominations warn against prophets and prophetic giftings. And I've actually heard media people mock the possibility of someone hearing God speak, both while interviewing a Christian and when simply referring to one.

I guess I can see how some unbelievers, ignorant of Scripture and having no relationship with God, might think people who believe they hear from the Lord are strange. They've probably met some of the ones I've also run into, the ones who approach me with a sort of spaced-out, super-spiritual, I'm-from-another-planet look and give me a message "from God" (a message usually as bizarre as their expression).

However, I do get a little puzzled by Christians who reject the possibility of God speaking to a person's heart, mind, or spirit. Most of these believe He spoke in Old Testament times and then stopped after He gave us the Bible. I'm not criticizing them or belittling their position, but it does seem strange to me that God would suddenly lose His desire or ability to communicate verbally, especially to His kids. I don't carry on a running conversation with God, and I've never heard His voice audibly, but I confess to being one of the "nut cases" that believes God talks to him at times. And I believe in prophets.

Back to the statement from the late '80s. I was having a fairly normal phone conversation with this brother when he began speaking to me prophetically. I don't remember much of it, but one phrase I have never forgotten was so unique, it stood out to me. He said God was going to bring forth "the fresh age of the Melchizedek order" and that I would be a part of it.

"What is that?" I asked when he concluded.

"I don't know," he said somewhat humorously. "But when you find out, let me know."

Fast-forward approximately fifteen years to October 2002. I was praying for America, primarily concerning the judicial system, when I heard the Holy Spirit clearly say, "You will fully shift the government of America when the prayer movement fully shifts from priestly intercession to kingly intercession as well." I suddenly remembered what the prophet had long ago said to me, the dots connected in my mind, and at last I understood "the fresh age of the Melchizedek order." Grasping this revelation will expand our understanding of governmental intercession.

There is rich and powerful revelation connected to Melchizedek in the Scriptures, but for our subject I'll skip over much of it. He is first mentioned in Genesis 14, again in Psalm 110, and then in the New Testament book of Hebrews. Some theologians think he was an Old Testament-era appearance of Jesus, others that he only symbolically pictured Christ. Of the latter we are certain as, indeed, it was said of Jesus that He is a priest "according to the order of Melchizedek" (see Psalm 110:4; Hebrews 5:6–10).

One fascinating fact about Melchizedek is that he was both a *king* and a *priest;* this was one of the ways in which he imaged Jesus, our King and High Priest. Zechariah 6:13 refers to this, stating, "It is He who will build the temple of the Lord, and He who will bear the honor and sit and rule on His throne. Thus, He will be a *priest* on His *throne*, and the counsel of peace will be between the two offices" (emphasis added).

It is important for us to understand the differences between these two functions. As our High Priest, Jesus represents us *to God.* For example, through Him we have forgiveness; it is through Him that we have access to the Father; He is the guarantee in heaven that we receive all the benefits He secured for us; and, being human himself, He can relate to and sympathize with our human weaknesses and temptations, thereby coming to our aid.

On the other hand, as King, Christ represents and releases the rule or authority of God from heaven *to earth.* In Psalm 2 the Father says, "I have installed My King upon Zion" (v. 6), then goes on to describe Christ's awesome power and authority. Jesus is not only King over the church but also over all the earth.

Here is a further summary of the differences between these functions:

- AS KING HE REPRESENTS THE RULE AND WILL OF GOD; AS PRIEST HE REPRESENTS THE NEEDS AND DESIRES OF PEOPLE.
- HIS KINGLY ROLE IS DOWNWARD, FROM HEAVEN TO EARTH; HIS PRIESTLY ROLE IS UPWARD, FROM EARTH TO HEAVEN.
- HIS KINGLY ACTIVITY IS GOD-CENTERED, HIS PRIESTLY ACTIVITY IS HUMAN-CENTERED.
- HIS KINGLY FUNCTION REQUIRES AUTHORITY AND POWER; HIS PRIESTLY ROLE REQUIRES LOVE, MERCY, AND GRACE.
- KINGS HAVE A SCEPTER THAT SYMBOLIZES AUTHORITY; PRIESTS USE A CENSER THAT SYMBOLIZES WORSHIP. ONE RELEASES POWER, THE OTHER A FRAGRANCE.

While we must comprehend these functions of Christ, we must also realize that as His body on earth He fulfills them through us. We are His voice, His hands, His feet. We are Christ's church, His legislature and, as such, partners in His mission and partakers of His anointing. What He is, He is through us; what He does, He does through us. It's not really complicated—we're partners, a team, a unit. Not equal partners, of course. As the Head, He's in charge; as the body, we serve the will of the Head.

Keeping this partnering and representational relationship with Christ in mind, we can grasp the fresh age of the Melchizedek order, in which we have become extensions of His King-Priest role. We too are called priests, and, as such, we're an extension of Christ in His priestly role, representing the needs of people *upward* to heaven. Just as Christ "*offered up* both prayers and supplications" while on earth (Hebrews 5:7, emphasis added), we also as priests "*offer up* spiritual sacrifices" (1 Peter 2:5, emphasis added).

AS HIGH PRIEST, JESUS REPRESENTS US TO GOD. AS KING, HE REPRESENTS AND RELEASES THE RULE OR AUTHORITY OF GOD FROM HEAVEN TO EARTH.

Jeremy was Miriam's teenage son who worked at a car wash. One Wednesday night Miriam had been driving home from a prayer meeting at her church, and as she drove she was fervently praying for her children. She was so engrossed in prayer that she didn't even look up when she passed the car wash to see if Jeremy was there.

Shortly afterward, Jeremy came home, badly shaken. "Mom," he said, "I saw you pass by while I was at the car wash."

"I'm sorry, Jeremy. I should have stopped."

"No, let me tell you what happened. At the very moment you passed by, a man had a gun at my head. It was a holdup. He said, 'Give me your keys and your money.' I said, 'Man, don't do this.' That's when I looked up and saw you pass by.

"When I looked back at the man, he was looking at me strangely, but not really at me. He was sort of looking past me, and it was as though he saw something or someone at my shoulder. All at once he turned and ran."

"Jeremy," said Miriam. "I was praying for you at that very moment."

"I believe you, Mom," said Jeremy. "I believe you."[1]

What an incredible example of timely, priestly intercession. Who knows what would have happened had Jeremy's mother not been praying for him at that dangerous moment.

Most Christians, though they may or may not think of it as priestly activity, realize that we send worship and prayer from earth to heaven. But most of us completely miss God's plan concerning our kingly anointing of representing Christ. We are not only priests, we're a "*royal* priesthood" (1 Peter 2:9, emphasis added).

Symbolically, we are seated with Christ on His throne (Ephesians 1:20; 2:6), told to reign in life (Romans 5:17); we are instructed to extend His scepter (Psalm 110:2) and are given keys of kingdom authority with which to bind and loose, forbid and allow (Matthew 16:19). We are kings and queens—royalty. And whereas priests "offer up" to heaven, kings "proclaim" downward to earth. Just as Christ decreed the will of the Father in situations—pronouncing blessings and curses, casting out demons, healing the sick, even raising the dead—we are told as royal priests to "*proclaim* the excellencies" of God (1 Peter 2:9, emphasis added).

What do we proclaim? "Excellencies" is the Greek word *arête*, also meaning "manliness, valor, superiority." One lexicon calls it "virtue as a force or energy of the Holy Spirit accompanying the preaching of the glorious gospel."[2] As representatives of King Jesus, we are called to proclaim the "superiority" of God. We have the privilege of releasing the "force or energy of the Holy Spirit" as we proclaim the good news of Christ.

I intentionally used the word *decreeing* to describe my actions in front of the White House. I was not so much asking God to do something, I was decreeing for Him His will. In the next two chapters we'll discuss this declarative facet of governmental intercession in detail. For now, I am simply highlighting that this is one of the ways we release kingly intercession.

Both the priestly and kingly dimensions of prayer can be seen through what we call "the Lord's Prayer" (Matthew 6:9–13 NKJV):

- THE PRAYER BEGINS WITH PRAISE, AN OBVIOUS EXAMPLE OF PRIESTLY INTERCESSION: "OUR FATHER IN HEAVEN, HALLOWED BE YOUR NAME."
- THE PRAYER THEN SHIFTS TO KINGLY INTERCESSION WITH IMPERATIVES: "YOUR KINGDOM COME. YOUR WILL BE DONE, ON EARTH AS IT IS IN HEAVEN." THE VERBS "COME" AND "BE" ARE BOTH IN COMMAND FORM (IMPERATIVE) IN GREEK. IN OTHER WORDS, WE ARE NOT ONLY TO REQUEST HIS KINGDOM RULE AND WILL—WE ARE TO DECREE THEM INTO SITUATIONS FOR HIM. KINGLY, GOVERNMENTAL INTERCESSION, BRINGING HEAVEN TO EARTH.
- THE PRAYER THEN SHIFTS BACK TO PRIESTLY PETITIONING, ASKING FOR PROVISION, FORGIVENESS, AND FREEDOM FROM TEMPTATION.

This pattern can also be seen in several of the psalms, Psalm 24 being a prime example. Beginning with priestly language, the psalmist starts with praise, then speaks about ascending into God's presence with clean hands and a pure heart, seeking His face (vv. 1–6)—all priestly activities.

Notice, however, the shift in verse 7: "Lift up your heads, O gates, and be lifted up, O ancient doors, that the King of glory may come in!" The direction changes from upward to downward as the activity shifts from priestly to kingly. Decrees and commands replace praise and communion. The psalmist commands gates to open so "the King of glory" can enter. He is representing "the Lord strong and mighty, the Lord mighty in battle" (v. 8), and in so doing he has shifted from humble praise to bold proclamations.

KINGLY INTERCESSION IS GOD'S ROYAL PRIESTHOOD REIGNING IN LIFE THROUGH THE AUTHORITY OF CHRIST.

Dick Eastman, president of Every Home for Christ, tells of a prayer that exemplifies just such a shift from priestly to kingly intercession. He and others were praying for the sale of their California headquarters building so they could move the organization to Colorado Springs. In Dick's own words:

> What happened next prompted me to look at my watch. It was 9:55 A.M. The intercessor who had been petitioning God for His intervention had completely changed the tone of his praying.
>
> He had been rehearsing in prayer certain factors God was certainly well aware of: the declining economic conditions of the city; recent articles in the local newspaper explaining how few, if any, office buildings were selling in the Los Angeles area; and the fact that our small street was lined with buildings for sale, some perhaps better and even cheaper than ours. What a faith-building prayer!
>
> But then came the change. The prayer seemed to take a quantum spiritual leap in boldness. It began with a simple phrase, "God, no matter the circumstance, You have just the right buyer for this building." Next came, "In fact, I believe You can see that buyer even now. You know his name. You can see where he is—what he's doing right now."
>
> What happened next I believe was a divinely initiated transition into the arena of prophetic prayer. The intercessor suddenly spoke directly to the would-be buyer, "I believe that even

now God sees you driving along the streets near the EHC office, looking for just the right building for your business." An even more startling directive followed, *"I command you to come forth now. Not tomorrow, not next week, not next month, but today."*

Remarkably, an older man with a young couple walked through the front door a few minutes after 10:00 A.M. Theirs would be the only offer on the property. The purchase was finalized exactly on time for that summer's move to Colorado Springs. And it had all begun with a prophetic prayer.[3]

What Dick calls "prophetic prayer" was also kingly intercession. It is God's royal priesthood reigning in life through the authority of Christ. As you intercede for individuals, places, or situations, the Holy Spirit will at times lead you to move into this type of prayer. When He does, be bold and respond in faith. Don't waver as I did at the White House. You do have kingly authority.

CHAPTER 8

THE VOICE

How forcible are right words! (Job 6:25 KJV*)*

Traveling to all fifty states with Chuck Pierce was a lesson in flexibility. In San Antonio, he ran to the platform, interrupted my message—yes, he interrupted my message—took the microphone, and began to prophesy.

The first time he did this was in our first state on the tour, New Mexico. There he didn't come to the platform, didn't say "excuse me," didn't wave to get my attention, didn't even stand up. They had given him his own mic, so when he decided it was time to prophesy, he just flipped it on and, right from his seat, took off.

Scared me half to death!

"Just give me a little warning, next time," I pleaded. "Wave, stand up, anything at all. Just give a little warning." So Chuck started coming to the platform when he felt led to interrupt my messages.

We actually operated this way often. Our purpose on this tour was not to teach, but rather to discern what God was saying, pray it, and decree it. Therefore, it was never truly an interruption, but a welcome accomplishment of our mission. Sometimes I would continue my message after he finished; other times we moved into prayers and declarations based on what he prophesied.

On this particular night in Texas, Chuck began to speak and in the course of the prophecy said that if we prayed, Saddam Hussein would be captured within seven days. Then he turned around and handed me the mic with an "I can't believe I just said that, you'd better do something" expression.

My first thought was, *Why are you handing me the mic? You got us into this situation, you get us out.* But it was too late—I had the mic and everyone was looking at me. I did the only thing I knew to do—pray. As I prayed, I began to move from priestly to kingly intercession. I discerned the Spirit leading me to command and decree that the demonic activity keeping Hussein hidden be broken. Other leaders came to the platform and offered similar prayers and decrees.

Saddam Hussein was captured three days later!

Kingly intercession is released through decrees. With them we "legislate" God's will on earth, in much the same way an earthly king would enact his. Chuck says the following about prophetic revelation and decrees:

> God has chosen us as the necessary link to bring His will from heaven to earth. He wants us to commune with Him, listen carefully to His voice, gain prophetic revelation, and decree that revelation into the earth. This will unlock miracles and release His blessings. Once we hear God, we can intercede, but we can also prophesy. Prophesying is declaring His mind and His heart. As we speak, He forms His will in the earth. We should always be willing to say "yes and amen" to His promises. When we receive prophetic revelation, we need to decree the prophetic revelation. This was the pattern that we operated in, once we gathered together in our meetings from state to state.[1]

There are two types of prophetic activity, and here Chuck alludes to both. Prophesying is more than *foretelling*—predicting the future. It is also *forthtelling*—speaking forth the plans and will of God for the present and the future. This is still classified biblically as prophetic because of the discernment required for us to know His plans and will. John the Baptist was called a prophet, yet as far as we know he did no foretelling or predicting future events. He *did*, however, discern the times and *speak forth* what God was saying about the present. Accordingly, this forthtelling aspect of the prophetic is also referred to as "prophetic intercession."

When Chuck and I met with intercessors and other church leaders in all fifty states in 2003–2004, our purposes were:

(1) to gather God's people for agreement and the resulting synergy;
(2) to discern Satan's strongholds over a given region and what caused them;
(3) to discern the Lord's strategies in order to break those strongholds, and also His strategy for how He intended to move the church forward toward revival;
(4) to release priestly intercession through corporate repentance and prayer;
(5) to release kingly, governmental intercession through prophetic decrees.

PROPHESYING IS MORE THAN FORETELLING—PREDICTING THE FUTURE. IT IS ALSO FORTHTELLING—SPEAKING FORTH THE PLANS AND WILL OF GOD FOR THE PRESENT AND THE FUTURE.

We never released the same prophetic words, decrees, or strategies for any two states.[2] In the Texas gathering where we decreed Saddam's capture, God had given me a word about the state's prophetic calling and destiny. When I said this meant God's purposes for America will sometimes be declared, launched, or pictured from there, Chuck began to receive a prophetic download. He heard the Spirit say, "Go to the platform and prophesy what I give you—and don't think about it." He knew later that he probably wouldn't have said it (about Saddam) had he thought about it first.

What prophetic dynamics occurred in the meeting that night? (1) *Prophetic discernment* of one of God's overall purposes for a state; (2) this prepared the way for a *prophetic word* concerning His specific desire at that moment; (3) the word prompted me to seek *prophetic instructions;* (4) these led us to release *prophetic decrees*, a type of governmental intercession, that is, legislating from the heavens. All of this worked together to become kingly intercession made by the *ekklesia*, the legislative body of Christ, ruling for Him on earth. It was kingdom authority releasing kingdom power, just as Jesus instructed us to do: "Your kingdom come, Your will be done!"

We and an army of intercessors moved in every state in this prophetic, kingly intercession; you need to do this from room to room in your house! You can and should release this type of intercession, not only for the world at large but also for your private and immediate world. Do it for individuals, your family, business, church, and city. Sit on the devil's chest!

What are decrees, declarations, and proclamations? Chuck says:

> A *decree* is an official order, edict, or decision. A decree is something that seems to be foreordained. This is what makes a decree prophetic. *Decree* can also mean to order, decide, or officially appoint a group or person to accomplish something. A decree is linked with setting apart or ordaining something or someone. A *declaration* is an announcement, a formal statement. . . . This statement is what a plaintiff sometimes releases in

> his complaint, which results in a court action. A *proclamation* actually brings something into a more official realm. A proclamation can ban, outlaw, or restrict. This is linked with the process of binding and loosing.[3]

Words, in general, are amazing. James, in chapter 3 of his letter, notes that with them we bless and curse. He goes on to compare the power of words to a forest fire, a fountain of life, a world of iniquity, and deadly poison. Strong words about the power of words!

Our opening verse from Job calls words "forcible." The Hebrew *morat* means "to press." One of its biblical uses describes a king pressing his seal of authority onto a decree or legal document with his signet ring, making it legally binding (the law of the land). Words seal deals and decree laws. They are powerful, even unto life and death (see Proverbs 18:20–21). The New Testament says we are justified or condemned by them (see Matthew 12:37).

- WARS ARE STARTED WITH WORDS.
- LOVE IS COMMUNICATED THROUGH WORDS.
- INSTRUCTION AND EDUCATION ARE SHARED BY WORDS.
- DECEPTION AND CONFUSION ARE PROPAGATED WITH WORDS.
- KINGDOMS ARE BUILT WITH WORDS.
- PEOPLE ARE CONTROLLED BY WORDS.
- LIVES ARE SHATTERED AND HEALED THROUGH WORDS.
- WORLDS ARE CREATED BY WORDS—THE EARTH WAS AND SO IS OUR PERSONAL WORLD.

That last one is pretty heavy, isn't it? But it's true. Words may very well be the most powerful conduit of authority and power in the world. God's *Let there be . . .* created the world and everything in it.

Ecclesiastes 12:11 says, "The words of the wise are as goads, and as nails fastened by the masters of assemblies" (KJV). Nails help us build, construct, assemble, and hold things together. So do words. The Master Craftsman used them to build the earth, the seas, the mountains, and all the other amazing elements and dimensions of creation. Hebrews 1:3 tells us He holds it all together by the power of His words and decrees!

Luke's gospel says that even the incarnation—God becoming human—was caused by a combination of God's words and Spirit. When Mary asked how she, a virgin, could have a child, the angel informed her that the power of the Holy Spirit would overshadow her and impregnate her with Jesus (1:35). Then he said, "Nothing will be impossible with God" (1:37).

This translation doesn't do justice to the strength of what the angel actually said. The most literal and accurate rendering is: "No word spoken by God is without power." What a claim this is, and what ramifications it carries for us. *Our all-powerful God infuses transcendent power into His words.* They become the carriers of His awesome strength.

In the Scriptures, God issues myriad decrees or declarations. Zodhiates says, "The Ten Commandments are actually ten declarations."[4] They are not the Ten Suggestions. When God issues a command or decree, it is earth's law. To violate one is rebellion against His authority and invites certain judgment.

God also calls His Word a sword with which He rules and judges. His declarations not only create and build but they also judge and destroy. They are both *constructive* and *destructive.* Consider the following: "Out of His mouth came a sharp two-edged sword; and His face was like the sun shining in its strength" (Revelation 1:16); "Repent therefore; or else I am coming to you quickly, and I will make war ... with the sword of My mouth" (2:16; see also 19:15, 21).

Some of God's decrees are to create or perform something in the present; others are declarations about the future. In Isaiah 46:9–10, God says of himself,

> I am God, and there is no one like Me, *declaring the end from the beginning* and from ancient times things which have not been done, saying, "My purpose will be established, and I will accomplish all My good pleasure" (emphasis added).

What an amazing God! He stands outside of time and looks ahead, declares the future, and eventually time catches up to His decree. How preposterous the fools who think they will outwit or overpower Him! Chuck shares the following story that illustrates God's ability to declare the future:

> When my son Daniel was seven years old he came to his mother and me with a question: "What is anthrax?" We both were astonished that a seven-year-old boy would ask such a question. My stepfather (Daniel's grandfather) had cows and land, so I assumed that he had mentioned the issue of anthrax occurring in a natural context. However, when my wife and I questioned Daniel over where he had heard the word "anthrax" he said, "The Lord spoke it to me and said it is coming to America." I explained to him what anthrax was. We have always been honest with our kids, so I just laid it all out on the line. This caused him to fear that it might come upon him. When he would touch something, he would immediately wash his hands. This threw us into a crisis as a family.
>
> In my quiet time one morning I began to seek the Lord, asking Him how He would pull us out of this awkward situation and bring freedom and confidence to Daniel. The Spirit of God said: "This will not be an issue in Daniel's life until he is 20 years old." At breakfast that morning when he began to obsessively discuss anthrax with us, I told him what the Lord had said. Pam gave me that look that said "Why in the world would you say this so I

have to live with his obsessive fear for the next 13 years?" Nothing really changed, except that I had heard God.

When I do not know what to do, I either worship or ask God what I can give. I find that I can begin to hear Him when I begin to worship, and He will always tell me where to give. Then I can hear Him on the issues that burden my heart. That night when I put Daniel to bed, I said to him, "Let's worship." We listened to an audiocassette and sang along. At the end of the music, I said to Daniel, "You know how much Mom and I love you. We have tried every way we know to help you get through the fear of what God has shown you. Perfect love casts out all fear. God does not give you the spirit of fear. Therefore, ask the Lord to show you how much He loves you. Since we've worshiped, is there anything you want to ask the Lord?" Daniel replied, "I've been trying to catch a butterfly all week, and I've not been able to."

As any good parent, I wanted to go out and find every butterfly I could and put them all in his room so that when he awakened, they would be surrounding him. However, I knew I could not do that. I had to trust the Lord. The next morning, when he got up and we were sitting outside, he still feared anthrax. While I was praying for him before I left for work, an interesting thing happened. A butterfly flew into our yard and landed upon Daniel's shirt. He cupped his hands around the butterfly and looked up at the Lord and said, "Because You have shown me how much You love me, I'm just going to set this butterfly free." This was quite a moment.

On Daniel's 20th birthday, the headlines in the newspapers in America read "Anthrax Strikes America." I was traveling and called him on his birthday. Remembering God's word about anthrax, I asked Daniel how he was doing. He said, "Dad, since we worshiped that night and God revealed His love to me the next day, I have never questioned His love protecting me in the midst of this particular crisis." He had received faith that would last him the next 13 years of his life and extend into the future.[5]

Thirteen years before they happened, God declared that the anthrax attacks would occur. I want us to see what happens when time catches up to the decree God makes concerning the future. What does He do at that point? He involves us in its fulfillment. *We become the voice of God in the earth, decreeing His decrees for Him!* Job 22:28 says, "You will also decree a thing, and it will be established for you; and light will shine on your ways." The first part could be more literally rendered "You will decree a decree." We discern God's will and decree—what He has determined about a given situation—and decree His decree.

WHEN TIME CATCHES UP TO THE DECREE GOD MAKES CONCERNING THE FUTURE, HE INVOLVES US IN ITS FULFILLMENT. WE BECOME THE VOICE OF GOD IN THE EARTH, DECREEING HIS DECREES FOR HIM!

The verse then says that when we decree the decree, it will be "established." This is the Hebrew word *quwm*, which means "to rise."[6] God's Word is called a seed (1 Peter 1:23), and when we sow it into a situation, we are sprinkling the seeds through which He causes His will to spring up. *Quwm* also describes a variety of other activities, including God's "creative, saving and judging action" rising up.[7] Our decreeing the Lord's Word releases His *creativity*, His *salvation*, and yes, His *judgments*!

Now a twist to the anthrax story. Chuck said his son would not face anthrax until he was twenty. Time did catch up to the decree from thirteen years earlier; God's decree did not create these attacks, but He knew they were coming and told Chuck. When they arrived, He used His people to decree against and stop them. Jim and Faith Chosa, powerful Native American prayer leaders from Montana, with New Jersey Strategic Prayer Network coordinators John and Sheryl Price, relate the details.

> Just after the WTC disaster on 9/11/01, unknown individuals began sending through the postal service, from somewhere in the city of Trenton, NJ, envelopes filled with anthrax. The effect on the nation, already in shock, was severe. And even more so in the state of New Jersey.
>
> However, spiritual mappers [those who understand how to discern the spiritual cause of certain natural events] within the prayer networks in New Jersey, were able to link the current event with an ancient bio-terrorism event perpetrated in 1763 by William Trent, the namesake of Trenton, NJ, against the Ottawa Indians who at the time were laying siege to Fort Pitt. Inspired by a British commander, William Trent had sent into the Ottawa camp two blankets and several cloths which were inoculated with the smallpox virus. The effect on the Ottawa people was devastating. The surviving remnant packed up and headed into the Ohio Valley carrying smallpox with them, increasing the terror for all people they came in contact with.

This unrepented sin was allowing Satan to visit on America the same type of judgment. (A biblical precedent can be found in 2 Samuel 21.) The Chosas and Prices go on to say:

> On November 1, 2002, we gathered in New Jersey with a united representation of the prayer networks of the state. Twelve Native believers participating in this event released the preemptive forgiveness of God to immigrant believers present, as they represented the immigrant bloodlines that perpetrated the act in 1763. We then removed from the spiritual landscape the defile-

ments of bloodshed and broken covenants caused by this act and, united with the Body of Christ as one, broke the ancient curse of bio-terrorism in the landscape.

The Anglo-American Body of Christ gave the Chosas, as representatives of the Native Americans, two blankets, again inoculated, but this time with praise and worship to God! The Anglo-Americans then mailed these blankets through the postal system to our address in Montana, in order to cleanse this system from any lingering effects of the bio-curse. The impact was immediate, resulting with no more anthrax attacks through the postal system from Trenton, NJ.

That, my friend, is kingly intercession! The power of God's inspired words is extraordinary. *He rules through words—and so must we.* In fact, you will never truly rule your world until you learn the force of words. Thank God for leaders and intercessors who understand this spiritual authority and know how to pray!

You too are a part of God's government on the earth, and He desires to decree His will and purposes through you. You are a member of His church—the *ekklesia*—and as such have authority to insist on His will and stop the plans of hell.

CHAPTER 9

The Sword

We have seen that awesome authority and power are released when God uses the church to decree His will over situations. This power releases both the Lord's salvation to His people and His judgments to His enemies. The following is one of the most amazing testimonies of this I have ever heard. God used Jay Swallow, Native American spiritual leader, and a team of intercessors to overthrow a spirit of suicide on the Sioux Standing Rock reservation. With Jay's permission, here is the story in his own words.

> Prior to my personal involvement in the recovery of the Sioux Standing Rock reservation to a more normal way of life, I had been keeping track of the percentage of suicides among the mostly younger generation of the members of the tribe. There had been dozens of suicides and attempted suicides over the past few years. Just in the last three months they had had six suicides and 31 more attempts. I, being a longtime visitor of the Reservation since 1968, and [having] seen many forms of revivals in all of the Districts that make up the community population of the whole Reservation, was fairly well known for my efforts to bring relief to this needy area of Indian Country.
>
> Back then as it is today, poverty is still the reason for the collapse of hope, especially among the younger generation. As we

know, this leads to alcoholism, drug abuse, child abuse, and many other problems. When added up, the ultimate relief was "suicide."

The atmosphere on the reservation was saturated with panic, not only in homes that feared their own children would be the next to take their lives, but also in the Tribal Government itself. More and more Federal programs were called on to bring relief, totaling a million and a half dollars. Social programs, prevention programs, health programs, judicial programs, welfare programs and youth programs of every description were major players in trying to bring back social order to the reservation. Instead, the suicides escalated out of control.

In October of 2001, I was contacted by Pastor/Evangelist Antoine American Horse, Jr. He sounded desperate and tired as he explained the suicide situation that was, in his own words, "completely out of control."

He stated that he had talked with the Tribal Chairman and the elected officials as well as the Supreme Court Justice, and they gave him full permission and authority to contact me to see if I could come and help resolve the problem. After a lengthy talk on the phone and a three-day time frame of seeking the Lord for my personal direction, I answered with a definite "yes." All I required was the complete authority to do things my way after I sought God for direction.

After being allowed for two weeks before my journey there to use the Tribal radio station that services three surrounding reservations, I spoke to leaders of all faiths and organizations to join with me in a conference to end the reign of terror by the spirit of suicide. One hour a day for a week we sought the attention of those that would join with me in the conference beginning December 27–29, 2001. We called it "The Summit Meeting on Suicide."

Between October and December I started an intense spiritual preparation for this mission. Needless to say, the warfare at times was almost overwhelming.

After assembling my team of five including myself, we were anointed and prayed over by the Oklahoma Concert of Prayer to separate us for this mission (Acts 13:2). We left Oklahoma early morning of the 26th of December. At approximately 3:00 A.M. on the 27th, we arrived at the Reservation line on the south end, which was actually in South Dakota.

We stopped long enough to serve notice to the strongman residing over the Reservation. Larry Brown, a man of great reputation and authority of blowing the shofar, sounded the battle cry of the ancient instrument of history past.

I, Dutch, want to insert here that, true to his nature, Jay is being humble. The spiritual authority he walks in is truly amazing. The hair on the back of my neck stood up and I had chills all over when I heard him tell this story. In this written report, he mentions stopping at the border of this reservation and blowing the shofar. What he does not say is that he then made a powerful declaration over the entire reservation. Jay bound the strongman, forbidding him and his demons from causing any more suicides until he and the team received further strategy from God—they would then give the strongman and his demons their final orders. My friend, that is faith—and that is authority!

The summit meeting started at 8:00 A.M. with registration. I was overwhelmed to see that 110 concerned leaders had heard my plea and decided that what I was proposing was probably better than all the previous efforts. After addressing the clergy of the various Christian organizations, I boldly told them they were responsible for the takeover of their reservation by another spirit. They all humbly agreed, repented, and reconciled with one another in front of a large number of non-believers. This itself was historical and later proved to be effective.

The next two days were very intense and the resistance in

> the atmosphere was very challenging. I thought my intercessors and I were the only ones that actually knew what we were dealing with and what we were after. But I found out that the anointing given to me for this occasion was understood clearly by those in attendance. On the afternoon of the 29th at 3:30 P.M., the Lord said, "Now is the time," I asked for the shofar to be blown into the heavens, and the strength and courage came to me as I began to dismantle the strongman over the Reservation. We were totally immersed into an atmosphere that I had not experienced before. The whole room and the people there were affected by the spiritual visitation. The assurance came to me. I, and those in attendance, knew we had cleared the atmosphere over the Reservation from the grasp of the strongman. This began the two year and ten month total absence of suicide attempts and actual suicides. The Reservation and its people were free and normalcy came back to the homes.[1]

Awesome! That is kingly intercession at its highest level—using the sword of the Spirit (Ephesians 6:10–17) to war against the powers of darkness. Isaiah 48 also speaks of God's words and the creative power of this partnership between Him and His people. Look especially at verses 6–7:

> You have heard; look at all this. And you, will you not declare it? *I proclaim* to you new things from this time, even hidden things which you have not known. They are *created* now and not long ago; and before today you have not heard them, lest you should say, "Behold, I knew them" (emphasis added).

Now notice verse 7 in the *Amplified:* "They are created now *[called into being by the prophetic word]*, and not long ago; and before today you never heard of them, lest you should say, Behold, I knew them!" God wills and proclaims His plan, then we are called to prophetically discern His will and timing and to prophetically decree it, which in turn releases His creative power to accomplish it.

Sandy Grady, an intercessor in Washington, D.C., was used in this way for the state of Virginia. She saw a situation that needed to change, then discerned God's plan and implemented it. Here is her story:

> In the early nineties, I noticed that a lot of focus was being drawn to the federal government for prayer and action, but very little attention was being given to the state governments.
>
> In working with the WallBuilders organization, I decided to use the state in which I live, Virginia, as a model for praying over state government. I knew very little about this state's government at the time, but after research, realized there was a desperate need of prayer for government leaders and for pro-family values in the Commonwealth. A majority of the legislative leaders were showing a great disrespect for the sanctity of life, prayer in schools, and other values that I held dear.
>
> After surveying the situation (using the Nehemiah pattern), I asked God for a prayer strategy. The Lord showed me to write a Proclamation over Virginia stating the present condition and what would happen when the citizens of Virginia prayed for His government to take over. This Proclamation went out all over Virginia, courtesy of many ministries. It seemed that everyone was in total agreement. At the first joint prayer meeting, the room was packed with intercessors from all over the state who had just been waiting for an invitation like this. The room we used in the Capitol was the very room where Patrick Henry and Thomas Jefferson had spoken in earlier years. Together we decreed this proclamation and continued to do so.
>
> Within one election year, the legislative makeup began to change to a more pro-life and pro-family friendly Assembly. The new administration welcomed prayer regularly in the Capitol and

in the Governor's Mansion. Prayer has continued each day on site during the General Assembly meetings since then, and we continue to add to the number of legislators who believe in and pass Godly legislation.

This is legislating for the legislature! It is God's kingdom government praying and decreeing into earthly government what is needed.

Ezekiel 37 is a striking biblical example of God ruling and creating through the decrees of a person. In this passage Israel's spiritual condition is seen in a vision as a valley filled with dry, scattered bones. In other words, Israel was spiritually dead. God's method of restoration was for Ezekiel to prophesy or decree to them:

> Again He said to me, "Prophesy over these bones and say to them, 'O dry bones, hear the word of the Lord.' Thus says the Lord God to these bones, 'Behold, I will cause breath to enter you that you may come to life. I will put sinews on you, make flesh grow back on you, cover you with skin, and put breath in you that you may come alive; and you will know that I am the Lord.' So I prophesied as I was commanded; and as I prophesied, there was a noise, and behold, a rattling; and the bones came together, bone to its bone" (vv. 4–7).

At this point, even though the bodies were now whole, there was still no breath in them. Again the prophet was told to prophesy, this time to the breath or Spirit of God to enter them. It would seem that God needed or required the prophet's involvement at every step of the process:

> Then He said to me, "Prophesy to the breath, prophesy, son of man, and say to the breath, 'Thus says the Lord God, "Come from the four winds, O breath, and breathe on these slain, that they come to life."'" So I prophesied as He commanded me, and the breath came into them, and they came to life and stood on their feet, an exceedingly great army. (vv. 9–10)

This is astounding—a human decreeing to and releasing the Holy Spirit! Note, however, that Ezekiel was not dictating *to* the Spirit but *for* Him. God was giving the orders. Ezekiel was partnering with Him, functioning as His voice on the earth. In verse 14, God says, "I, the Lord, have spoken and done it." He refers to the prophet's words as His own—and indeed they were, for they carried His authority and released His power. Several characteristics of God's Word that we examined in the last chapter are here in this powerful account. God's words through the prophet:

- WERE FORCEFUL (JOB 6:25 NKJV).
- HAD THE POWER OF DEATH AND LIFE (PROVERBS 18:20–21).
- WERE WELL-DRIVEN NAILS—(ECCLESIASTES 12:11).
- WERE NOT WITHOUT POWER (LUKE 1:37).
- ESTABLISHED GOD'S WILL (JOB 22:28).

Jeremiah's ministry is another vivid portrayal of God releasing His words through a person: "Then the Lord stretched out His hand and touched my mouth, and the Lord said to me, 'Behold, I have put My words in your mouth'" (1:9).

Next, God told him what they were going to do: "See, I have appointed you this day over the nations and over the kingdoms, to pluck up and to break down, to destroy and to overthrow, to build and to plant" (v. 10).

After this Jeremiah records, "Then the Lord said to me, 'You have seen well, for I am watching over My word to perform it'" (v. 12). Please don't miss this: God's words, which He intended to watch over and perform, were going to be those He spoke through a human being, as verses 16–17 bear out one more time. "I will pronounce My judgments on them. . . . Arise, and speak to them all which I command you."

The pattern could not be clearer: God's Word, but spoken through people. This has always been the way He has operated. Hosea 6:5 states: "Therefore I have hewn them [My people] in pieces by the prophets; I have slain them by the words of My mouth; and the judgments on you are like the light that goes forth." God's decrees and judgments, released by a person's words.

You may be thinking, "Yes, but that was all Old Testament." God's method of operation hasn't changed! The New Testament also speaks of God releasing His judgments through our declarations. Recall the passage in which Jesus speaks of His *ekklesia* (church), which we defined as His parliament or governing body on earth. Look at the *Amplified* Matthew 16:19:

> I will give you the keys of the kingdom of heaven, and whatever you bind—that is, *declare to be improper and unlawful*—on earth must be already bound in heaven; and whatever you loose on earth—*declare lawful*—must be what is already loosed in heaven (emphasis added).

(Incidentally, after this verse, the *Amplified* references Isaiah 22:22, which I used at the White House, about governmental authority to open and close doors.)

Here Jesus tells us, as His government on the earth, to declare—*based on God's will and Word*—what is lawful and unlawful, allowed and disallowed. Seemingly incredible, but also reasonable, for how could we govern on God's behalf without such authority?

IN ORDER TO BE EFFECTIVE, THE CONTENT OF OUR DECREES MUST BE WHAT GOD DESIRES.

The following account pictures both the Lord's judgments released against His enemies, as He did through Jeremiah's words, and the bringing forth of His plans and purposes. I want to stress that these "enemies" are the powers of darkness, not people.

I have prayed in and around various government buildings on numerous occasions. One of those was on June 16, 2005, at the Supreme Court. I had been given a five-point prayer assignment by a trusted friend and intercessor, Jay Comisky. Jay told me he had received five biblical declarations over the Court while praying and that he had envisioned me decreeing them there.

My schedule was extremely full, with no windows for a trip to D.C. However, I believe very much in Jay's credibility, in the power of Spirit-led decrees, and in God's calling on my life. So I rearranged my schedule and on my next ministry trip routed through D.C. in order to fulfill this assignment.

I felt that rather than going inside the Supreme Court building, I was to make these five decrees from the outside, once on all four sides. I did this and in a couple of hours was on my way. Decree number two was that God's shifting of the Court was changing from a "siege" to a "suddenly." I had no idea what this meant, I simply decreed it the way Jay received it.

This is an important point. We must not inject our understanding or wishes into an assignment from God. We must be very careful to do and say what He instructs. I'm not implying that we have to hear God's decree word for word and say it in exactly that form. But in order to be effective, the content of our decrees must be what *God* desires.

As I stated, I had no idea what the "suddenly" was, but two and a half weeks later Sandra Day O'Connor resigned. No one expected it—most (including me) thought Chief Justice William Rehnquist would be first. But the "suddenly" did come, and I knew it was from God.

My assignment for the "suddenly" wasn't over, though. Twice since, I have been back to D.C. to pray about this appointment (and will be going again soon). One of those trips was three days before President Bush nominated John Roberts.

Knowing that President Bush was under great pressure to appoint a moderate rather than a strong moral and constitutional conservative, I felt I was to go to the White House and pray for him. I did so with Lou Engle and Sandy Grady. We were there simply as "tourists," not by official invitation. We walked through the White House for approximately an hour, praying for God to lead the president in his decision and decreeing that only God's choice would be made.

During this time, something strange kept occurring. Sandy, one of the most tuned-in intercessors I know and an intercessor on D.C.'s behalf for thirty years, kept bringing up horses. She said she kept thinking about horses when she prayed, and then she kept being drawn to pictures and sculptures of horses in the White House.

We could not discern what this was about, but we knew God was trying to direct us. Again, it is not necessary to have exact words and phrases in order to speak for God. He is not legalistic. He requires our involvement, obedience, and prayer—not perfection in our verbal delivery.

Believing God was saying something but not knowing what it was, we offered a prayer that went something like this: "God, You are obviously drawing our attention to horses. We don't know why and it makes no sense to us. But we declare that Your plans and purposes concerning "horses" and this Supreme Court decision will be fulfilled. We decree that Your kingdom will come and Your will be done." Then we continued praying for the president and various facets of his decision.

I must confess that it seemed very foolish praying about horses, but the three of us have learned to obey even when we don't understand. Imagine our pleasant surprise a few days later when we read the following teaser: "How a quartet of power brokers known as the Four Horsemen is shaping the future of the high court."[2] A portion of the article stated:

> The men, who have been dialing in [to the White House] since 2003, have come to be known as the "Four Horsemen": C. Boyden Gray, Edwin Meese III, Jay Sekulow, and Leonard Leo. Hand-picked by the White House for their ties to disparate conservative groups, they have been instrumental in helping the president name strict constitutionalists to the federal bench—and now they hope to do the same on the nation's highest court. "We've been waiting for this for four years," says Sekulow of the American Center for Law and Justice. And so the Four Horsemen are galloping into this confirmation fight.

WE ARE GOD'S PLAN!

We didn't know the president's four advisors were called "the Four Horsemen." We simply prayed and decreed that God's purposes concerning the court decision would be fulfilled and that the "horse" part of it, whatever it was, would be taken care of. We now know we were praying for wisdom to be given to them and the president as they worked together on this issue. We believe that happened, and that Supreme Court Justice Roberts was the right choice.

We are God's plan! He is waiting for the church to be the *church*—functioning as His parliamentary council, legislating His will through Spirit-led decrees, frustrating the councils of hell. He is waiting for us to command His will over the lives of individuals and declare that they will not be destroyed by Satan's schemes. If you're a true Christian, you're a part of this great governing body. Don't wait any longer to begin extending God's rule into the earth.

CHAPTER 10

THE HEAVENS

Blessed be the God and Father of our Lord Jesus Christ, who has blessed us with every spiritual blessing in the heavenly places in Christ . . . which He brought about in Christ, when He raised Him from the dead, and seated Him at His right hand in the heavenly places . . . and raised us up with Him, and seated us with Him in the heavenly places, in Christ Jesus . . . so that the manifold wisdom of God might now be made known through the church to the rulers and the authorities in the heavenly places. . . . For our struggle is not against flesh and blood, but against the rulers, against the powers, against the world forces of this darkness, against the spiritual forces of wickedness in the heavenly places. (Ephesians 1:3, 20; 2:6; 3:10; 6:12)

This sounds like one uninterrupted passage of Scripture, doesn't it? I became fascinated one day as I read these verses consecutively with none of the in-between sections. When I saw how well they flowed together, I realized they really do provide a continuity of thought. In summary, they tell us we have been given everything we need in order to operate in heavenly places; Christ has been given all authority in this realm; we have been seated there with Him in that position of authority; through us, from our position there with Christ,

God intends to deal with the kingdom of darkness; finally, the last verse describes that evil kingdom, listing its various components.

What are "heavenly places"? This is not referring to heaven, God's home, but to the invisible atmosphere all around us. We must understand this relatively unknown dimension in order to fully partner with God and experience the fullness of His blessing. This is the unseen realm of the spirit—invisible yet real, hidden yet very active. Much of what happens on earth is influenced by it; certainly anything of eternal significance or regulating the destinies of people and nations is controlled within it. Most people, including Christians, give little thought to the unseen world governing the one we see. Many, especially in cultures that emphasize higher education and intellectualism, are actually cynical of this arena. But the Bible is filled with descriptions and accounts of it—in fact, this is the story of Scripture. Apart from it, there is no God, Satan, angels, demons, fall of humankind, birth of Christ, redemption through the cross, miracles, or resurrection of the dead. Yet again, surprisingly, most American Christians live their lives without weighing how much this realm affects us, let alone how we can influence it.

Here is a significant truth: *The more we learn to function in the invisible spiritual realm, recognizing and applying its governing principles, the more we can partner with God, positively impact our world, avoid the snares and influence of the evil one, and enjoy the blessings of our salvation.*[1] As I meditated on the Ephesians verses, God began revealing to me that I was not conscious enough of this realm. It was not a new subject to me. I have comprehended it for many years and realized that we can influence it through our prayers and actions. But the Holy Spirit began revealing to me that I was not as aware of this dimension as I needed to be.

I saw clearly that if I was going to be as effective as I could be in changing situations on earth, I had to understand how this heavenly realm affected it. Conversely, I also needed greater understanding of how I could influence the invisible world. And hopefully do all of this without becoming weird!

The more I meditated on this spiritual sphere, the more I realized it is the Bible's major theme—two invisible kingdoms warring for control of the world. If we could see what takes place around us in this realm, we would no doubt see a great kingdom clash—angelic and demonic forces engaged in phenomenal warfare. I don't know exactly what it looks like, but I know it goes on. The following vivid account of the unseen gives us a glimpse:

> When the attendant of the man of God had risen early and gone out, behold, an army with horses and chariots was circling the city. And his servant said to him, "Alas, my master! What shall we do?" So he answered, "Do not fear, for those who are with us are more than those who are with them." Then Elisha prayed and said, "O Lord, I pray, open his eyes that he may see." And the Lord opened the servant's eyes, and he saw; and behold, the mountain was full of horses and chariots of fire all around Elisha. And when they came down to him, Elisha prayed to the Lord and said, "Strike this people with blindness, I pray." So He struck them with blindness according to the word of Elisha. (2 Kings 6:15–18)

The invisible forces were there all along—it was just that Elisha's servant could not see them. And so it is with us. We live in a world filled with constant and tremendous angelic and demonic activity. Our natural eyes simply cannot perceive it.

It amazes me how many Christians, though they claim to believe the Bible and would say they believe in these "heavenly places," still have a problem consciously relating to it. Many, for example, take issue with any form of prayer dealing with demons, angels, or invisible strongholds.

The world, of course—those who do not profess to be Christians—has an even greater problem acknowledging the invisible spiritual realm. The very suggestion of an invisible sphere influencing the visible world elicits immediate skepticism (or mockery) and often an inference that anyone who believes in this realm is not in touch with reality.

What a boost for the devil's activities!

But at some point, if we are going to be truly effective in prayer, especially governmental intercession, we must acknowledge, understand, and learn to influence the spiritual realm. We must move beyond our fear of what others think, and agree with Scripture. Jesus is our example, and He frequently dealt with the invisible. He was always aware of it and consistently engaged unseen entities, stirring up demonic opposition everywhere He went.

The early church in Acts did so as well, confronting forces of darkness and dealing with them when appropriate. We are inconsistent if we confess to be Bible-believing followers of Christ and yet refuse to acknowledge and deal with the invisible kingdom of darkness. Failure in this area has rendered us largely impotent.

This account, which demonstrates our need to become involved in the spiritual arena, also shows kingdom authority being dramatically released.

> Some of our staff, along with students from our ministry school, have gone a number of times to a nearby university that is a major center of New Age spiritualism. The most popular religion on campus is witchcraft. My senior associate [Kris], a wonderfully anointed prophet of God, was invited to speak in a class on Christianity and the supernatural. He stood before the students and shared a brief testimony. At the end of the class a young lady who was tormented by demons began to manifest under their influence. Kris commanded them to leave, and she was delivered in front of many wide-eyed students! She was then

> filled with so much joy that they had to carry her out of the classroom into the parking lot so the next class could begin. The students from both classes looked on at what was happening, stunned and dumbfounded. My associate began to call people out, pointing at them and speaking strong prophetic words into their lives that touched the secret things of their hearts. Some dropped to the floor instantly as if they'd lost their strength. Others sat there with their mouths gaping. "I saw you being dedicated to God," he told one young man who was the only unbeliever in a large family. And on it went until those witches and warlocks who had devoted their lives to the powers of hell knew there was a mighty God in Israel, and in the Church![2]

This is the church being the church. We must grow in our boldness and skill, learning to partner with the Spirit to operate in and impact this realm.

Another Old Testament passage, Exodus 17, demonstrates this invisible war in Joshua's leading the Israelite troops into battle against the Amalekites. God told Moses to go up on the mountain overlooking the battlefield with the rod He had given him and to hold it aloft. This rod symbolized God's authority in much the same way a king's scepter represents his; it had been so throughout Israel's deliverance from Egypt, always representing His authority, which released His power. Raising the rod, Moses was exalting God's strength.

Scripture tells us that when Moses' arms became weary and he was no longer able to hold up the rod, the battle would turn against Israel. When his hands were held high with the rod extended, the battle would go in Israel's favor. This was obviously not an issue of morale. The soldiers were not watching Moses while engaged in conflict. The cause of the momentum swings was completely separate from their conscious minds. It was the invisible war in the heavens.

While there were *visible*, flesh-and-blood people fighting with tangible, physical weapons on a very real battlefield, the action of Moses on the mountain was releasing an *invisible* force determining the conflict's outcome. Notice that both realms were actually influencing the other: (1) Actions occurring in the *visible* realm [Moses lifting the staff] (2) activated God's *invisible* authority and power, (3) which in turn, determined the outcome in the *visible* realm (the battle). Each arena—natural and spiritual, seen and unseen—still affects the other today. Millions of good and bad events occur on earth every day due to this two-way cause and effect.[3]

Daniel 10 records an example of angels serving Daniel in an extraordinary angelic visitation with a remarkable message from God.

> Behold, a hand touched me and set me trembling on my hands and knees. And he said to me, "O Daniel, man of high esteem, understand the words that I am about to tell you and stand upright, for I have now been sent to you." And when he had spoken this word to me, I stood up trembling. Then he said to me, "Do not be afraid, Daniel, for from the first day that you set your heart on understanding this and on humbling yourself before your God, your words were heard, and I have come in response to your words. But the prince of the kingdom of Persia was withstanding me for twenty-one days; then behold, Michael, one of the chief princes, came to help me, for I had been left there with the kings of Persia. . . ." Then he said, "Do you understand why I came to you? But I shall now return to fight against the prince of Persia; so I am going forth, and behold, the prince of Greece is about to come" (vv. 10–13, 20).

Daniel, a man of passionate prayer, had cried out to God for several things, one of which was Israel's restoration. As incredible as it sounds, the angel that appeared said to him, "I was sent to you the first day you began to pray, but I was opposed by a spirit called the prince of Persia."

In late October 2004, just a few days before the presidential election, I lived an experience somewhat similar to Daniel's. In fact, his story influenced mine. Unlike Daniel, I didn't see angels, but they were there. I should have known better than to try to take a vacation the week before an election. I'm usually engrossed in prayer at that time, but on this occasion I felt the election would go the way the Lord wanted.

A few days before the end of my vacation, however, I became very troubled. I sensed a great increase of spiritual warfare over this election. Satan must have brought in demonic reinforcements from all over the world to try to turn it toward his desired end. The burden on me was so great I knew I had to go to D.C. to pray. I have been there to pray just before every major election for the past eight years, so that in itself was nothing new. The suddenness and interruption was what made this trip unique.

Ceci and I decided she would go home to Colorado Springs and I would catch a flight to Washington. She knows the assignment on my life and knew the importance of this vote, so she was fully supportive. Later that night, an intercessor in Colorado Springs, Timmerle DeKeyser, called me. She said, "One of the other intercessors in the church had a dream about you last night, which I felt you should know about immediately. She dreamed she was attending a conference and went into an average-sized room for the first teaching session. There was a man standing up front, ready to begin teaching, with a large media screen behind him. As he started to teach, he turned to this intercessor and said, 'Tell Dutch Sheets he must go up to 11 and 12.' On the screen behind him, the numbers 11 and 12 appeared as he said this.

"In her dream the scene changed and she was in another room for another session. The same man was there to teach, and again he looked at her before he began and said, 'Tell Dutch Sheets he must go up to 11 and 12.' This ended the dream."

I took this call while in the lobby of a music hall; Ceci had gone in to get our seats. As I walked in, pondering, I saw Ceci waving, and I made my way over. Entering our row, I noticed it was row 12, but darkness kept me from seeing seat numbers. "What seats are we in?" I asked her.

"Row 12, seats 11 and 12," she said.

"I think God is talking to me!" I said and then related to her the dream. Indeed, He was.

I began to seek the Lord as to what these numbers meant. Why was He saying I must go up to 11 and 12? Why would this be given to me on the eve of my trip to Washington to pray for the upcoming elections? My first thought when seeking direction is always to look in Scripture, so I began to look up references with 11 and 12 in them.

I felt drawn to Matthew 11:12: "From the days of John the Baptist until now the kingdom of heaven suffers violence, and violent men take it by force." I contemplated this verse and discerned that God was indeed giving me prayer insight for the Washington assignment.

I also looked at Revelation 12 and realized it's all about spiritual warfare. God's angel Michael and other angels were warring against Satan, the dragon. I found verse 8 particularly interesting: No room was found any longer in the heavens for the dragon and his angels. I realized God was confirming to me that there was great warfare over D.C. and that I was definitely going there to participate in it.

What a way to end a vacation!

I was especially encouraged by verse 11—until I got to the last phrase, that is: "for they did not love and cling to life even when faced with death" (AMP).

Meditating on Revelation 12, I received a call from a different Colorado intercessor, Jean Steffenson, who said, "I have been praying for you and felt strongly led by the Holy Spirit to ask you to read Daniel chapter 10. God wants to speak to you from there."

As I read and meditated, I realized the chapter also includes a story about Michael warring in the heavens, this time against a spirit called the Prince of Persia. Daniel had been praying and God had dispatched angels with an answer, but demonic forces in the spiritual realm were warring against the angels bringing him the answer. God sent Michael to help the other angels break through to Daniel.

While meditating on this, I suddenly remembered a prophetic exhortation given to me a few months earlier. Jane Hamon, while speaking in our church, prophesied that sometime in the near future God was going to send the archangel Michael to war over D.C. and I was going to go and partner with him.

I had forgotten this word. Probably on purpose! But after reading about Michael warring in the heavens in Revelation and Daniel, I remembered. God was telling me, "I have sent you here to Washington to war against Satan's strategies to control this election, and I am sending Michael to help you."

I am very grateful for the prophetic gifting God has placed in the church. If not for this dream about the numbers 11 and 12, I would not have been reading Revelation 12 and would not have remembered the prophecy about warring alongside Michael in D.C. Because of these occurrences, however, I and several others asked God to send Michael and a host of angels to help us in this battle. The result was immediate and incredible. In my life I have never been in a room where the atmosphere changed more quickly and dramatically. I knew Michael and his angelic force had come.

As one final encouragement for this assignment, the Lord led a member of Congress to call me just before I left for the White House. "How are you feeling about the elections?" he asked.

I explained what had transpired while on vacation, where I was, and what I was about to do. "Perhaps you're supposed to pray for me and with your governmental authority send me, in a spiritual sense, into this assignment," I suggested.

"I believe so," this legislator said, "because you just came to mind and I felt impressed to call you immediately." The prayer was powerful and added greatly to my confidence.

I and three others had a powerful prayer time at the White House for an hour or more. We bound the efforts of Satan to determine the election's outcome. With many petitions and decrees we released kingly, governmental intercession. We commanded God's kingdom rule to come and His will to be done in the upcoming days.

We believe our prayers were answered. Of course, there were thousands of believers around the nation also praying concerning these elections, and we are certainly not trying to take the credit. We were only a part of the efforts. But sometimes the Lord needs someone to go to the heart of the battle and make His decrees. When I do this, I see myself as the point of a spear or arrow, with all the prayers of God's people being the shaft and bow. All of it is necessary.

There is one further significant interpretation of the 11 and 12 dream, relating to biblical symbolism of the numbers 11 and 12. I should add at this point that I would never base doctrine on the interpretation of numbers, nor would I ever take action based only on it. However, God does use the symbolic meaning of numbers in Scripture. No serious biblical scholar questions this. I don't want to bore you with a lot of theology, so I'll simply give you enough reference to assure you of this pattern. The number three, for example, represents resurrection; five is the number of grace. Seven pictures completion and rest, as in the Sabbath; eight symbolizes new beginnings.

In this biblical numbering system, the number 11 refers to a change of paradigm or a transition from one place or way of thinking to another. It can also picture disorder, because there is often a temporary season of disarray or disorder during a transition. The number 12 is the number for kingdom order and government. For example, the crown in Revelation 12:1 had twelve stars, probably referring to the twelve tribes of Israel; 21:14 speaks of the wall of the New Jerusalem having twelve foundation stones, which had on them the names of the original twelve apostles of Christ.

Through these two numbers I felt God was saying to me, "You must go through the disorder (11) in the heavens and exercise My kingdom government or rule (12)." As you can imagine, with so much confirmation and orchestration by the Spirit, I fulfilled this assignment with great confidence, knowing I was obeying God's direction and moving in His authority.

CHAPTER 11
THE ROOM

Dad, I had an interesting dream last night," said my youngest daughter, Hannah. Knowing she receives dreams from the Holy Spirit on occasion, I was anxious to hear the details. After I did, I knew it wasn't just for Hannah, but also for the body of Christ in general. And without any question, it was for me. Though some details are not pertinent to our subject, others are.

In her dream we were dropping her off at a college or university. The first thing she had to do was get new shoes. We went into a store named "Safeway," a supermarket chain in many parts of the country, and found the ones she needed. In her dream, she thought it was unusual that the shoes were found in a supermarket, so she looked back at it as we left. The name was no longer "Safeway" but "Other Things."

As we sought the Lord for interpretation, we felt the Spirit was saying there is a new phase or season coming (new shoes) and that on this journey we would not be able to go the "safe" and familiar way—He was about to do "other things." We would need to leave our comfort zones and be stretched into new methods and activities, all of which would require us to think differently.

When given her room assignment in the dream, Hannah was told she was in a particular building on "Gray Floor." That the name was a color was interesting and significant.

"What do you think that means?" she asked.

Knowing that gray hair is biblically symbolic of the wisdom that comes from age—the same Hebrew word meaning "old age" and "gray hair" *(siyb)* is also translated "elder" (see Ezra 5:5, 9; 6:7–8, 14)—I knew immediately that the floor's name symbolized wisdom.

Then she said, "Dad, when they gave me my room it was number 601. I know that seems strange, but it was very clear in my dream—601."

Instantly I knew what this meant also. With my love of word studies, I have examined the Greek for "revelation" *(apokalupsis)* enough to remember its number in Strong's numbering system for New Testament words. The number of this term's verb form ("to reveal") is 601; 602 is the number of its noun form.

Fascinated and amazed, I replied, "I know what it represents, Hannah—revelation. You were assigned the room of Revelation on the floor of Wisdom." Immediately I thought of Ephesians 1:17, "that the God of our Lord Jesus Christ, the Father of glory, may give to you a spirit of wisdom and of revelation in the knowledge of Him."

Hannah continued. "Dad, when I opened the door you were inside. Surprised, I said, 'Sorry Dad, I thought this was my room.'"

"It is," I had said to her in the dream. "I've been staying here, but now I'm giving it to you."

This dream carried great significance for me. I knew it indicated a new work God was about to do in our nation and a new phase of ministry for me. I believe He is beginning something very new in Hannah's generation, a move of the Spirit that for some time I have known in my heart was coming. I am convinced there is an imminent revival for America, starting with Hannah's generation, then spreading to all age groups. Through the dream God was instructing me to help father

her generation, giving wisdom and the revelation I have received.

The symbolic designations of her room and floor—which one was wisdom and which was revelation—were intriguing. The broader area (the floor) was wisdom, yet it wasn't complete without revelation (the room). Neither would be adequate or functional without the other. Revelation, spontaneous and specific understanding or strategy for current situations, must be interpreted in the larger context of wisdom, a general understanding of God's ways, purposes, and principles learned over time. *Every floor of wisdom must have a room of revelation; and every room of revelation must be found on the floor of wisdom.*

REVELATION, SPONTANEOUS AND SPECIFIC UNDERSTANDING OR STRATEGY FOR CURRENT SITUATIONS, MUST BE INTERPRETED IN THE LARGER CONTEXT OF WISDOM, A GENERAL UNDERSTANDING OF GOD'S WAYS, PURPOSES, AND PRINCIPLES LEARNED OVER TIME.

Most of the church focuses on one or the other—not a balance of the two—and I think it is fair to say that the greater portion of Christ's body focuses on the need for wisdom and knowledge. While I would never downplay the need for wisdom—in the dream it was the larger portion (an entire floor is obviously bigger than one room)—it is also true that wisdom without revelation is very detrimental to our cause.

What is revelation? It is more than simply gaining intellectual knowledge we didn't previously have. It is an understanding originating from the heart or spirit, revealed to us by the Holy Spirit.

The following verses make this clear:

> [I pray] that the God of our Lord Jesus Christ, the Father of glory, may give to you a spirit of wisdom and of *revelation* in the knowledge of Him. I pray that the *eyes of your heart* may be enlightened, so that you may know what is the hope of His calling, what are the riches of the glory of His inheritance in the saints. (Ephesians 1:17–18, emphasis added)
>
> Even if our gospel is veiled, it is veiled to those who are perishing, in whose case the god of this world has blinded the minds of the unbelieving, that they might not see the light of the gospel of the glory of Christ, who is the image of God. For we do not preach ourselves but Christ Jesus as Lord, and ourselves as your bond-servants for Jesus' sake. For God, who said, "Light shall shine out of darkness," is the One who has shone *in our hearts* to give the light of the knowledge of the glory of God in the face of Christ. (2 Corinthians 4:3–6, emphasis added)

It is inarguable that the biblical concept of revelation is not of the mind and does not originate with ourselves. The words *veiled (kalupto)* in the latter passage and *revelation (apokalupsis)* in the former come from the same root. The basic concept of *kalupto* is to hide or conceal something by covering or veiling it. Adding the prefix *apo* means to undo or reverse that process, giving us the concept of revelation. Simply stated, revelation is when God lifts the veil created by sin from our hearts and allows us to receive insight or understanding directly from Him.

Highlighting some of the differences between wisdom and revelation will help us understand their different roles. Wisdom is formulated based upon truth learned in the *past;* revelation, on the other hand, produces *present* truth and makes our wisdom relevant. Revelation brings *current strategy for current situations;* wisdom enables the *implementation of that strategy with skill.* Wisdom generates *consistency and balance;* revelation *prohibits stagnation.*

Note several potential ramifications of emphasizing one without the other. If we operate in wisdom without current revelation, we might:

- BECOME AN "OLD WINESKIN" (MATTHEW 9:17). (AN OLD WINESKIN DOESN'T REFER TO A PERSON WITHOUT TRUTH BUT TO ONE WITHOUT "PRESENT TRUTH" [SEE 2 PETER 1:12]).
- KNOW RIGHT PRINCIPLES BUT FALL SHORT IN THEIR PROPER TIMING AND APPLICATION.
- EMPHASIZE THEOLOGY AND DOCTRINE WHILE LACKING POWER (TRUTH OVER SPIRIT).
- EMPHASIZE INTELLECT OVER GIFTS OR POWER, FORMULAS OVER THE SPIRIT'S DIRECTION.
- BECOME RELIGIOUS—OUTWARDLY DISPLAYING CHRISTIANITY WITHOUT POWER, PUTTING FORWARD ROUTINE WITHOUT RELATIONSHIP.

If on the other hand, we overemphasize revelation and/or underemphasize wisdom and understanding, we have the potential of:

- NOT PLACING ENOUGH IMPORTANCE ON SOUND DOCTRINE.
- BECOMING TOO SUBJECTIVE IN OUR APPROACH TO LIFE AND SPIRITUALITY.
- MISINTERPRETING AND MISAPPLYING THE REVELATION WE RECEIVE.
- PRIORITIZING POWER OVER TRUTH, SPIRIT OVER WORD.

Since there is a far greater emphasis in the church on wisdom and learned knowledge, contrasted to what I believe is a great lack of revelation, I want to focus the remainder of my comments in this and the next chapter on the need for and benefits of revelation, *in the context of praying with authority.*

Kingly, governmental intercession is absolutely linked to revelation. We can never be confident we are operating in God-given authority if we are not certain we are functioning according to His will and strategy.

> This is the confidence which we have before Him, that, if we ask anything according to His will, He hears us. And if we know that He hears us in whatever we ask, we know that we have the requests which we have asked from Him. (1 John 5:14–15)

REVELATION IS WHEN GOD LIFTS THE VEIL CREATED BY SIN FROM OUR HEARTS AND ALLOWS US TO RECEIVE INSIGHT OR UNDERSTANDING DIRECTLY FROM HIM.

My first thought when praying about any situation is usually *What Scripture applies to this?* or *Holy Spirit, what is Your will and strategy in this matter?* Our greatest lack in prayer is allowing the Spirit to help us. Jesus said it was to our "advantage" that He leave the earth, for if He did not, the "Helper" would not come (see John 16:7). *Helper* comes from a Greek word meaning "one who comes alongside to give aid." We don't press our advantage—the Holy Spirit—enough in prayer.

Jesus went on to say of the Spirit that He would "disclose" things to us (vv. 14–15). While not the same Greek word as revelation, the term used for disclose, *anaggello*, is equally important and revealing. The prefix *ana* means "back," and *aggello* means "to announce";[1] "possibly the *ana* carries the significance of upward, i.e., heavenly, as characteristic of the nature of the tidings. To tell in return, bring word back."[2]

The significance is obvious and cannot be overemphasized. The

Spirit, our Helper, wants to bring us heavenly counsel and strategy, disclosing God's plans to us. It should be obvious that to whatever degree this occurs, to that degree we will have success. Proverbs 16:3 (AMP) agrees: "Roll your works upon the Lord—commit and trust them wholly to Him; [He will cause your thoughts to become agreeable to His will, and] so shall your plans be established and succeed." The following story illustrates the role of our Helper and the success that comes when we allow Him to help us.

> A young man named Brandon, who is a graduate of Bethel School of Supernatural Ministry, was visiting friends in Washington State. They were at a restaurant and the waitress came to take their order. Brandon began to perceive things in his heart about the woman, and he shared them with her. They pertained to her relationship with her mother. The waitress was amazed, and she became so emotional that she had to take a break.
>
> While the waitress was away, Brandon noticed an Asian couple staring at him from across the room. The woman had wrist braces on because she suffered from carpal tunnel syndrome, and one of her hands was completely frozen in a fist. Brandon walked over and asked if he could pray for her. She said that they were Buddhists, but they were willing to receive prayer. He prayed for her and she was healed on the spot. The whole family was instantly overjoyed and began praising Jesus, right at their table. They said they had been praying to their ancestors for a long time for her hands to be healed, but the prayers hadn't worked. Brandon explained who Jesus is, and they received the gospel with wonder and thankfulness. He went back to his table and for the rest of the evening, the healed woman sat there opening and closing her hand in amazement.
>
> About that time, the waitress came back and asked if she could talk with Brandon outside. She was understandably confused and yet eager, and wanted to know more about God.

Brandon shared further insight that the Holy Spirit gave him about her life and told her about Jesus' love. She gave her heart to the Lord and was filled with the Holy Spirit right there. She was breathless with excitement and declared she was going to tell all of her friends what had happened.[3]

Without disclosure from the Spirit, neither the salvation of the waitress or the healing of the Buddhist would have occurred. Governmental intercession discerns the will of the King in heaven and insists on it being accomplished on earth. God loves the lost and desires to demonstrate that love. The Holy Spirit desperately wants to help us make the demonstration.

God speaks to us in many ways. Scripture is absolutely the primary and only infallible method He uses, the standard by which all other revelation must be judged. But God does speak to us by His Spirit, directly to our hearts and minds, and through supernatural methods such as dreams, visions, and prophecy. He also uses circumstances. Regardless of His chosen method, hearing from God is not optional if we are to be overcomers in life. The following testimony of Lou Engle's assistant and intercessor, Brian Kim, illustrates just how willing God is to disclose to us His direction and strategy.

> Since July 2002, I have been on a Daniel-type fast, eating no meats or sweets (Daniel 8:1–16) for the ending of abortion and for justice and righteousness to be restored in America. After President Bush, who was clearly pro-life, was reelected in November, I wanted to end the fast and eat meats and sweets again. So the morning after it was official that President Bush had won the election, I prayed to the Lord and said, "Lord, I want to end this fast today, so if you don't give me an indication that I am to stay on this fast, I'm going to eat cake tonight."
>
> Throughout the day, I continually prayed and asked God for confirmation if I was to continue on the fast. At 10:00 P.M. that

night, I went to meet one of my college friends to study and when I arrived in the library I noticed a young man already studying with my friend. I walked up to the young man I did not know and introduced myself saying, "Hello, I am Brian Kim." The young man responded saying, "Hello. I am Daniel Fast."

How's that for divine revelation! In this situation, God chose not to speak directly to Brian's heart but rather to use an amazing set of circumstances. I know Brian personally. He continued the fast and now lives in the D.C. area, giving himself to prayer and fasting for the ending of abortion and the release of revival. Brian is a member of the emerging generation that will live on the floor of wisdom in the room of revelation.

Sometimes finding our personal room of revelation is a process, requiring time and great perseverance. After several years of tragedy, pain, and loss, the Smith family in my congregation shares their testimony of God's faithfulness and ultimate victory.

My husband Steve and I were married in 1984 and we have five beautiful children. Just before our son Zack turned eleven, he was diagnosed with a rare form of children's cancer and given a 20 percent chance of a five-year survival. He went through years of chemotherapy and radiation, had 32 surgeries and made it through a stem cell transplant. His leg was eventually amputated at the pelvis.

We all fought, none harder than Zack. At times I had such faith that things would be okay, at other times fear that they would not. On April 16, 2003, he went home to be with Jesus. At first Steve and I felt relief that his suffering was over, but then the guilt and depression set in. I felt so guilty, wondering if I prayed hard enough. A deep sadness came over me and I thought I was going to die from it at times.

We experienced depression and disappointment, anger,

tormented sleep, and enough tears to drown in. Our hope, peace, and joy were all taken from us. Even our very identity was gone—our whole life had been wrapped up in Zack and his illness. Sometimes people would not even call me by my name but say, "Hey, are you Zack's mom?" It was the same for all of us.

Another problem became a complicating factor. Finances have always been a problem for us; it seemed like we were always going around the same old mountain. Making ends meet often seemed impossible. As is typical in situations like ours, Steve and I were even starting to grow apart, each in our own little corner dealing with things in our own way. After Zack passed away I started working to help make ends meet and even that did not seem to help. It seemed like there was always something coming along to steal from us so we could never get ahead.

Then in March of 2005 Steve lost his job. He carried so much guilt. He applied for several jobs, and one that looked promising was a welding job, something he had not done in years but was trained to do. To our great disappointment, however, he did not pass the test. He took a job at Wal-Mart, making much less than before and hating it.

I had finally had enough. I knew we had to do something. All the depression and hopelessness was getting the best of Steve and me. We were the picture perfect—*unhappy*—family. There was no joy, no hope—things I should have found joy in I did not. I wore a façade, but inside was miserable. We decided we needed help. Restoring the Foundations, a model of prayer and deliverance based on a combination of Scripture and Spirit-led prayer was suggested to us. I was afraid, because to do the program meant opening up and letting go of so many things, but I went ahead with it anyway. It is hard to let God do such a deep surgery. Healing often hurts, especially when things need to be cut out. Steve was also hesitant but went through the program as well.

Things began to change. Hope and peace were starting to come into our home. The atmosphere began to change as God was being put in His rightful place of authority and as Steve and I were willing to let God have the things that were separating us from Him. He had always been there but we had given other things and strongholds more authority than Him.

One week before we were to finish RTF Steve got a call from the welding place. They wanted him to try again, so three days after we finished RTF the test was scheduled. I had lost my position at work and was again stressing out a little, but Steve was different this time. He and the kids began to pray for me. My kids were prophesying and Steve was praying with more spiritual authority than I had seen in him in years.

The next day Steve went for the weld test and told me not to worry, he was going to get the job. God and I talked a lot that morning and I was still unsure about my not working. I told God that if He wanted me to be a stay-at-home mom, that Steve not only needed the job but I also told Him what Steve needed to make! Not only did Steve get the job, he was hired at almost 20 percent more than I asked for!

When a shift took place in Steve and me, everything changed at home. It became a totally different place. Not only did God show himself to be our provider, He restored so many things. I have joy unspeakable. There is peace, laughter, and hope for each new day. Steve and I are praying together. Our kids are praying again and on fire for God. There is more worship in our home than television. Our healing is ongoing, of course. God gracefully and gently encourages us forward. We will always miss our son, but where there was a deep, bleeding wound, God has brought healing and given us a peace.

It is amazing that when God is given His rightful place of authority He comes running with open arms, wanting nothing more than to bless and restore all that was lost. The enemy still

> tries to defeat us but the Lord says all things are possible if we believe. Our new family motto is, "A problem is really not a problem at all; it is just an opportunity thrown in our path to give God praise and testify to His greatness." Our lives have truly been turned around. There are really no words to describe what I feel in my heart. The sun seems to shine brighter and there is no heaviness in my heart, only joy and peace.

The transformed Smith family is an amazing inspiration to me. Many elements came into play in their story of triumph over tragedy. Of course they went through an unavoidable grieving process, but they ultimately had to make a conscious decision to allow God to bring them out of it. And more was needed than just the decision—discernment and revelation were required for them to know how to break free from their pain and current lack of provision. This came through skillful discernment and prophetic insight. Wisdom was required to apply that revelation in an appropriate and healing way. As they stated, they had to rise up and place God "in His rightful place of authority."

God wants you also to find your room of revelation. No matter how difficult your situation, the Holy Spirit is willing to disclose heaven's strategy and insight to you, enabling you to get Satan and adverse circumstances off your chest. Your destiny is to be a kingly warrior, overcoming in life through the kingdom authority of Jesus Christ.

You can do it!

CHAPTER 12

THE INTERRUPTION

We were in Florida on the Fifty-State Tour when Chuck interrupted my message. As usual, something I said awakened the prophetic anointing in him. I don't know how he functions in meetings without me.

"There is a terrorist cell in Tampa," he said in the course of his prophecy.

Again he handed me the microphone with a do-something-about-it look. Almost as if he were saying, "I found it. Now you deal with it."

I did the only thing I knew to do—pray. I led, while those present joined with me in agreement. We decreed that the terrorists would be found. Two weeks later a professor at a Tampa university was exposed and arrested as the leader of a group that funded Islamic terrorists.

That is warring by interruption and revelation!

In Matthew 16:18, Jesus speaks of building and warring by revelation. The context is that Peter has just received a powerful revelation of Jesus as the Messiah, the Son of God. Jesus commended him and said, "Upon this rock I will build My church." *The Amplified Bible* makes it clear that Jesus (1) was talking about spiritual warfare and (2) was not saying He would build His church on Peter, but upon the rock of revelation:

> I tell you, you are Peter [Petr*os*, masculine, a large piece of rock], and on this rock [petr*a*, feminine, a huge rock like Gibraltar] I will build My church, and the gates of Hades (the powers of the infernal region) shall not overpower it—or be strong to its detriment, or hold out against it.

Regarding "the gates of Hades," I love Kenneth Wuest's Translation, "the counsels of the unseen world shall not overpower it." Jesus then made His famous promise of giving us the keys, or authority, with which to bind and loose in the invisible realm called "heavenly places."

Far too often we try to build the church and war against Satan's plans and counsels without revelation—the counsels of heaven. This is futile, and our lack of success in many areas is the fruit of it. God, however, has been restoring our understanding of the need for the prophetic anointing that brings discernment and revelation. This is changing everything.

One of my favorite verses relating to the need for and power of revelation is 1 Chronicles 12:32: "Of the sons of Issachar, *men who understood the times, with knowledge of what Israel should do,* their chiefs were two hundred; and all their kinsmen were at their command (emphasis added)." *Times* in this verse is a Hebrew word meaning strategic or opportune times. (For those who enjoy word studies and know the Greek word *kairos,* this is the Hebrew equivalent.) These were men of revelation, and it was this revelation of the times that brought them knowledge of what to do.

We must realize this is a passage about war—the passage is often referenced, but that aspect is usually overlooked. Verse 1 introduces the upcoming list of David's mighty men with "they were among the mighty men who helped him in war." At the chapter's conclusion, we're again reminded that all these men were warriors (v. 38). Please don't miss the significance of this. This prophetic anointing—the ability to understand the times, which brought knowledge of what to do—had to do with war. This is instructional: For us to be effective in our *spiritual* war, we too must have an ability to discern the times. And like these men of old, from that revelation we can receive strategy.

This Hebrew word for "understanding" the times is also significant. This is more than a *learned*, intellectual knowledge or wisdom; it is *prophetic* revelation or discernment—a spiritually imparted knowledge. Several other passages where the same word is used will confirm this:

GOD IS NOT SAYING WE SHOULD ABANDON WISDOM OR COMMON SENSE. HE IS TELLING US NOT TO RELY ON OUR OWN HUMAN DISCERNMENT OF WHAT TO DO.

- IN 1 KINGS 3:9, SOLOMON ASKED GOD FOR AN ABILITY TO "DISCERN."
- IN DANIEL 1:17, 20, DANIEL WAS GIVEN THIS KIND OF "UNDERSTANDING" TO INTERPRET VISIONS AND DREAMS.
- IN 8:15–16, DANIEL ASKED FOR "UNDERSTANDING" TO INTERPRET A VISION.
- IN 9:22, DANIEL WAS GIVEN "INSTRUCTION" AND "INSIGHT WITH UNDERSTANDING" BY AN ANGEL. (I FIND THE PHRASE "INSIGHT WITH UNDERSTANDING" FASCINATING. I EQUATE IT TO "WISDOM AND REVELATION" IN EPHESIANS 1:17, WHICH WE DISCUSSED IN CHAPTER 11.)
- IN 10:1, DANIEL RECEIVED "UNDERSTANDING" TO INTERPRET A VISION FROM GOD.
- AND IN PROVERBS 3:5, GOD SAYS, "DO NOT LEAN ON YOUR OWN UNDERSTANDING."

Proverbs 3:5 makes much more sense when understood in this

light of prophetic revelation. God is not saying we should abandon wisdom or common sense. He is telling us not to rely on our own human discernment of what to do. "Receive revelation from Me," He is saying. Again, placing this understanding into the context of war (1 Chronicles 12) makes it especially significant. If we are to know what to do to overcome in spiritual warfare, we must receive spiritual revelation.

In October 2003, Chuck and I held our state meeting in Kansas. During this meeting, Chuck prophetically called the state to hold a worship gathering in Wichita, where worship would go forth to war against abortion. Wichita has become a leading national abortion center. Chuck said abortion is a sacrifice issue and the only thing that would successfully counteract it is worship.

Earl Pickard, U.S. State Strategic Prayer Network prayer coordinator, waited for the Lord to show him the right timing, and then in obedience to the God-given strategy, he conducted the worship gathering in Wichita. Here is the chronology of what occurred, along with the fruit, as reported by Jeff Kahrs.

On March 7, 2004, a twenty-four-hour worship service was held in Wichita, Kansas, to break the stronghold of abortion and death over Wichita. This time of worship was called by Chuck Pierce during the fifty-state tour held in Kansas last fall and was later organized by Earl Pickard.

On March 17, 2004, the noted serial killer BTK resurfaced for the first time in twenty-five years. (January 11, 2004, had marked the thirtieth anniversary of his first killings—the Otero family. He later went on to kill a total of ten people, but had not been heard of since 1979, and was assumed dead by most people—including the Wichita police department.)

Shortly after the BTK resurfaced the Lord revealed to me (and to my sister-in-law) that the enemy was very upset over the focused and intensified prayer and worship going out over Wichita in order to break the stronghold of abortion and death over our community. . . and thus brought the BTK out of hiding to instill fear throughout our community. Over the next eleven months the BTK began a series of bizarre and cryptic communications with the police department and the general public.

The Lord also impressed upon me the importance of prayer and that the local Christian community would have to "pray-in" the BTK before he was captured . . . that the powers keeping him concealed were very strong. I, along with others, I am sure, encouraged the believers to pray and press into the Lord for his capture. I took every opportunity I had to meet with area Christian leaders and preachers who loved the Lord and encouraged them to direct their congregations to pray for the capture of the BTK. I am quite sure many others were doing the same thing.

On January 11, 2005, a city-wide prayer meeting was called and organized by two prominent evangelical pastors in Wichita: Joe Wright of Central Christian Church and Terry Fox of Immanuel Baptist Church. The purpose of the prayer meeting was to pray for the capture (or surrender) of the BTK, pray for the healing of the victims' families, and pray for the healing of the community. Between fifty and one hundred people attended, including a representative of the local city government, city police department, and family members of the victims.

On February 25, 2005, the BTK was captured by local police authorities. This is less than one year after he resurfaced but more than thirty-one years after he committed his first serial killing.

No one can prove that the worship gathering brought the BTK killer out of hiding or that the prayers of the saints caused him to be captured. To the skeptic it will all be coincidental. But to those who believe in the power of prayer, the facts and chronology of the events speak for themselves. This was warring by revelation!

Paul told Timothy to "fight the good fight" by using "the prophecies previously made concerning you" (1 Timothy 1:18). David warred against the Philistines by receiving divine revelation (2 Samuel 5:23–25). Elijah overcame Jezebel through God-given revelation and strategy (1 Kings 17–18).

In 2 Chronicles 20, Israel defeated an invading army through receiving heavenly strategy. A prophet named Jahaziel gave them divine revelation for the battle (vv. 14–17). Listen to King Jehoshaphat's instructions to Israel before the battle: "Listen to me, O Judah and inhabitants of Jerusalem, put your trust in the Lord your God, and you will be established. Put your trust in His prophets and succeed" (v. 20).

If Israel had to listen for God's strategy from heaven in order to win their battles, isn't it reasonable that we will need to do the same in our spiritual warfare? To fail in this is to be defeated.

The Scriptures actually equate a lack of revelation to judgment. In Luke 12:54–56 and 19:41–44, Jesus rebuked the Pharisees and Jerusalem's religious community for not being able to understand or discern the times. Because this was caused by the hardness of their hearts, they received great judgment instead of blessing. He said to Jerusalem, in essence, "I wanted to send you a mighty visitation, but because you could not understand the times, you could not receive what I wanted to do" (see 19:44). Lack of revelation caused loss of God's visitation.

In verse 42, Christ also said that a part of their judgment was a further loss of revelation! His plans for them would be "hidden from [their] eyes." Because they refused to receive His current revelation, there was a greater inability to discern placed upon them. God began to intentionally hide things from them. What a terrifying thought.

Another similar judgment is pronounced in 13:35. Because the religious rulers had rejected the prophets, God said to them, "Your house is left to you desolate." This Greek phrase literally says, "Your house is left to you." In other words, God's judgment to them was, "You are now on your own. You rejected My prophetic anointing; you did not want My words. Therefore, that is exactly what you are going to get—you will be left with your own." Fearsome judgment!

There is an attitude within certain elements of the church that opposes the prophetic anointing, just as these early church leaders did. This is extremely dangerous. When we reject the prophetic anointing, we are rejecting a facet of Christ himself. He *is* our prophetic anointing. According to Revelation 19:10, the testimony of Jesus is the spirit of prophecy. Ephesians 4:7–12 tells us that the prophetic office and anointing is one of the five anointings of Christ.

WHEN WE REJECT THE PROPHETIC ANOINTING, WE ARE REJECTING A FACET OF CHRIST HIMSELF. HE IS OUR PROPHETIC ANOINTING.

Not to belabor the point, but 1 Samuel 3:1 is still another verse that lets us know a lack of revelation can be God's judgment. "The boy Samuel was ministering to the Lord before Eli. And word from the Lord was rare in those days, visions were infrequent." Because of the apostasy and sin of the priesthood, God had refused to release revelation in Israel. Because Samuel was a true worshiper, however, this was all about to change. God was lifting the curse and rebirthing a season of fresh revelation.

A prayer effort the Lord called me to a few months ago is another good example of how He uses revelation to lead us in spiritual warfare. As you will see, God went to great lengths to get the revelation to me. The saga began with a dream a young friend of mine, Crystal Hamon, was given in the latter part of 2003. Here are the primary details.

> Lou Engle and Dutch were together, in a building used for banquets and other gatherings. Lou was talking to people around him about prayer and fasting and was growing frustrated that they were not listening to him, but rather were just chattering and eating. Dutch, on the other hand, was talking to individuals and they were listening to him.
>
> The scene changed and Dutch approached Lou, handed him something I could not yet see in the dream and said, "Here, Lou, if you will strike this, they will listen to you." Dutch also handed him a conductor's wand with which to strike the unseen object. Lou did as instructed and a sound reverberated through the room. When the sound was heard, everyone began to pay close attention to him.
>
> When Lou turned back around to Dutch in the dream, what he was striking could be seen—it was "the scales of justice." He then looked at him and said, "This will crescendo on March the first."

As we, like Daniel, sought the Lord for insights concerning the dream, we received some we felt were significant. The scales of justice obviously referred to the courts. That the scales had to be struck evokes intercession (the Hebrew word for intercession is *paga*, "to strike the mark.") The conductor's wand indicated agreement, since the Greek word for agreement is *sumphoneô*, from which we get our word "symphony." That Lou and I were together and I handed him these things obviously indicated a need for our partnering in this.

In obedience to the revelation brought through this dream, Lou and I sent a letter asking intercessors associated with us in the prayer movement to fast and pray for a shift in the Court for forty days. Interestingly, backing up forty days from the day the dream said everything would crescendo—March 1—was Inauguration Day for President Bush's second term. Many people responded and joined us in prayer.

Here is when things got really interesting. At the end of the forty days, I was scheduled to minister in England. The night before I was to leave, February 27, I looked at the expiration date in my passport and realized I had been reading the date wrong for the last few years. The date was written in two different languages, and it had confused me. My passport had expired! I couldn't believe it. I felt foolish, embarrassed, and angry—and I was in a panic. I couldn't believe I was doing this to the people who had scheduled me for their conference. *I just have to get there*, I thought.

Both Ceci and Hannah had a different reaction. They told me from the very moment I realized my passport had expired that God was somehow in it. I did not accept this and said, "No, it's just my stupidity. I can't believe I did this. How could I be so stupid? I'm not a novice traveler. I should know how to read these things. How could I have misread this date for the last couple of years?"

"No," Hannah—who is very prophetic—said adamantly. "God is in this. You be alert to what He is doing."

I arose early the next morning, the day I was supposed to leave, and called the phone number I had for the U.S. Passport Agency. "How can I get a passport renewed quickly?" I asked.

"You will have to call one of the U.S. passport offices [she listed approximately ten cities], see if you can get an appointment, fly there, walk through the process, and if there are no problems, they will issue you a new passport," she told me. "But it is hard to get an appointment on short notice. Most of them are booked several days, sometimes even weeks, ahead."

Great, I thought.

I knew I would be at least a day or two late for this conference—if I made it at all. But since I was the keynote speaker for the latter half, I realized I might be able to get there for most of my teaching slots. If, that is, I could get an appointment in one of the passport-issuing cities, secure the necessary flights to it, and then get booked on new flights to England!

I then asked, "Of all of the passport office cities you have mentioned, which one would you recommend I try to get an appointment with?"

She thought for a moment and said, "I think you should try Philadelphia."

I hung up, called Philadelphia, and, to my surprise, they had an opening at nine the next morning. When calling them, there was no opportunity to talk to a person, so I could not plead my case or beg for a time slot. What was available on the computerized schedule is all that was offered, period.

I was able to route myself into Philadelphia late that night in order to be at the passport office the next morning. I was also able to get a new flight to England for the afternoon, should I be successful in renewing the passport. On the way to the office that morning I noticed, to my surprise, that it was only a block away from the Liberty Bell and Constitution Hall, where our government was formed. I have prayed there many times, and it is a very special place to me. As I rode in the taxi, I found myself thinking: *Wouldn't it be wonderful to spend some time praying here today?*

An hour or so later, while filling out my forms, suddenly I realized as I wrote the day's date that it was March 1, the last day of the forty days of prayer for the courts—Crescendo Day. In the panic of the last two days, I had completely forgotten. *What a shame*, I thought. *Here it is Crescendo Day and instead of praying, I'm distracted by this mess. Wouldn't it be great if I were here to pray instead of dealing with this situation?* Then I actually thought, *Wouldn't it be interesting if I ended up with time to go to Constitution Hall and pray? Could it be that Hannah was right and God wanted me to be here? No, I won't have any time to pray. This will take all morning, then I have to rush from here to the airport to catch the flight to London—if I even get my passport in time. No, I wish I were here for that reason, but it won't happen.*

After my forms were completed and I was called to the counter, the agent took all my information and said, "You have two hours now to wait. Go find something else to do for the next two hours."

"Don't I need to stay here?" I asked.

"We don't want you to stay here," she said. "Please go and return in two hours (at 11:00)."

As her words sank in, I began to sense God's presence in a strong way. Chills went up and down my spine as I sensed the Spirit's anointing coming upon me. Suddenly I knew in my heart all of this really was arranged by God. He had caused me to misread the date so He could get me to Philadelphia to pray on the Crescendo Day of this assignment. I still did not know, however, exactly what He wanted me to do.

First, I walked to the Liberty Bell and began to decree over America the verse written on it, Leviticus 25:10: "You shall thus consecrate the fiftieth year and proclaim a release through the land to all its inhabitants. It shall be a jubilee for you, and each of you shall return to his own property, and each of you shall return to his family." Then I went to Constitution Hall and signed up for a tour in order to go inside and pray through the building. When the tour ended, I knew my assignment still wasn't accomplished, but didn't know exactly what remained. I kept asking the Lord, "What do You want me to do?"

I continued to walk by myself around the outside of the hall, praying but not discerning what the Spirit wanted me to do. Finally, as I was about to leave the premises, I saw an adjacent building I had never entered. In all of the times I had been to this place, I had not even noticed it. While walking around praying, I had actually seen one or two people go in and out and wondered what it was, but there was no sign over the door and absolutely nothing to indicate its purpose. I felt the Spirit's prompting and kept hearing in my heart, *Go in there.*

I decided to obey, not even knowing if I actually was allowed to do so. Inside, I found a guard and a courtroom, which I could tell was very old and preserved in its original state. Inside, I again began to feel an incredible anointing and a great sense of destiny. (I have this hard-to-explain-feeling when on a strategic assignment from the Lord.) I asked the guard, "What is this place?"

"This is the original Supreme Court," he said, "where it all started."

I could not believe what I was hearing and replied in astonishment, "Are you telling me this is the birthplace of the Supreme Court of America?"

"Yes," he said, "this is where it began, in this very room."

I was speechless. I knew that at that very moment Lou Engle, my counterpart in the dream, was with a group of young people at the current Supreme Court building, "striking the scales of justice" through intercession. And here I was, the other man in the dream, standing in the original Supreme Court of America on Crescendo Day. In God's amazing sovereignty, He had orchestrated this series of events to get me to the place where our nation was born and our judicial branch was started. While Lou was decreeing God's will at the current Supreme Court, I was going to the root.

I realized I was on a very holy and important assignment. God had sent me there to "strike" the Supreme Court of America, decreeing His Word over it and commanding a return to its original intent. I knew I was there to call it back under God and to a fear of the Lord . . . to command it to become once again a government institution that would not try to expel God from public life in America but would welcome and honor Him. I was then to decree that it become again a court that would honor life and morality. Very quietly and while looking like nothing but a tourist I did these things, commanding God's kingdom to come, His will to be done, and a rebirth of His purposes for the Supreme Court of America.

Crescendo Day!

Do I really believe God orchestrated all of this and that my words made an impact? Absolutely! And we have now begun to see the changes. I realize it is not just because of my prayers but thousands of others as well. As is often the case, however, God needed someone to go and issue His divine decree.

God gave a young lady a dream. He gave Lou and me the interpretation of the dream. And then, in His sovereignty, He interrupted a trip overseas and motivated a passport agent who had no idea what was happening to advise me to go to Philadelphia. He opened a slot for me to be there at just the right time and led me to a building I did not even know existed—all in order that His purposes might be decreed over the place. Then He got me to my meeting on time—I never missed a session. What a God! And what evidence of His need and desire for us to represent Him in kingly governmental intercession.

Do not underestimate the importance of prophetic revelation. Your Helper is waiting to disclose God's will and strategies to you, and He will do whatever is necessary to make it happen. Ask for His help.

His "interrupting revelation" is waiting.

CHAPTER 13

THE LEVELS

I did pretty well in math—almost went into accounting. This was obviously an anomaly, because I can't seem to follow the simplest arithmetic when the three ladies in my life come home from a shopping excursion. Though I still do not understand the math, I am confident of the right question when they arrive: "How much money did you save me?"

I once made the idiotic mistake of asking, "How much did this cost me?" I received a quick lesson in protocol and Math 101.

So when Hannah (sixteen) came home last night from shopping with her mother, she started in immediately telling me how successful it was. "Great," I said. "How much money did this save me?" She rattled off the original price of each garment, then the sale price, announcing at the end of the list that she had just saved me $150.

I was ecstatic. So was she—and very proud of me. "You've made a lot of progress in understanding how this works, haven't you, Dad?"

"Absolutely."

Though I don't really understand this form of accounting, I realize that God made the female species with superior math skills. I am also very aware that my ignorance has caused an erosion of authority when it comes to shopping. There are other areas of our family life in which

I do have great authority—the TV remote, the garage, and the trash, for example.

It is a common misconception that all Christians have the same amount of authority to operate in Christ's name. We do not. There are several principles that will determine the varying degrees of spiritual authority we operate in as followers of Jesus (none of which have anything to do with math or shopping, by the way). I want to mention seven principles in this chapter and the next. Grasping this won't solve the confusion surrounding the male-female shopping breach, but knowing them will eliminate some confusion about prayer.

We Are One in Christ Jesus

The first principle that determines our level of authority in prayer is simply *our relationship to Christ—our salvation.* While each believer moves in differing levels of authority for some activities, everyone has equal authority to access the Father in Jesus' name. No Christian has any more authority to go before the heavenly Father than you do. No one has more access to the provisions procured for us by Christ than you. God has no second-class children. We all stand on equal ground and have the exact same potential level of authority when it comes to petitioning the Father in Jesus' name and requesting of Him the biblical promises made to us.

Notice that I used the word *potential* in the previous sentence. While we all have equal access to our heavenly Father in Christ's name, there are factors that can alter this. They have to do with our obedience to His Word and our freedom from sin. These can and will affect our right to approach the Father for His blessings.

The Bible is filled with passages indicating that our level of authority and favor with God is linked to our level of purity. Psalm 24, a striking example, tells us that those who have clean hands and a pure heart can approach God and His throne (see also 1:1–3; 1 John 1:5–10). We must not be deceived into believing we can do as we please, live contrary to God's laws, and still be welcome before our Father, let alone move in significant intercessory authority for others.

In Revelation 2 God addressed the church at Thyatira about their compromise with the spirit of Jezebel. He was angry with them because they were tolerating this spirit; He challenged them to change this, then said in verses 26–27, "He who overcomes, and he who keeps My deeds until the end, to him I will give authority over the nations, and he shall rule." God unquestionably links our authority level to our purity level. If we choose to compromise or allow a particular evil spirit to operate in our life, it will diminish the level of authority we possess, both when petitioning the Father for ourselves and for others.

Samson, of course, is another good example. His compromise with Delilah eventually eroded his authority and power and cost him his ministry, his freedom, his eyesight, and yes, his destiny. Our obedience to the Lord absolutely determines our rights before Him.

Circles of Authority

The second principle regarding our level of authority is what I call the principle of concentric expansion. Picture a small circle with ever-expanding circles around it, much like a target with larger and larger circles around the bull's-eye. For our discussion, the inner circle would represent us as individuals. As the circles expand and grow larger, they include more people and greater territory. As this increases, our authority decreases, since we are sharing it with others. The second circle might represent an individual's family, the third their city, the next their nation, and so on. Again, as the circles expand outward, our personal authority decreases.

No one has more authority over your life than you do. No one has greater authority to pray for you than yourself. We are born with a free will, the right to choose, and as we mature into adulthood this freedom increases. As far as God is concerned, no one can take it from us. With it, however, comes not only authority but also responsibility. Back in the late 1970s and early 1980s, I had numerous warts on my hands—as I recall, between thirty and forty. I had spoken with doctors, who were hesitant to remove them because several were next to my fingernails, some of them actually eating into the nail. On my right index finger I only had half a fingernail. Several cuticles were gone, having become one huge wart. They were irritating and embarrassing.

I had sought the Lord earnestly, asking Him to heal me, and I had fulfilled most if not all biblical procedures for healing. I had called the church elders to pray for me (James 5:14–15). I'd had hands laid on me according to Mark 16:18. I had other individuals who agreed in prayer with me (Matthew 18:19–20), I had been in services where the gifts of the Spirit, especially the gifts of healing, were manifesting in a pronounced way (1 Corinthians 12:9). I could never seem to receive my healing.

One day the Lord spoke to my heart very clearly: "I am never going to heal your hands based upon someone else's prayer or faith. You must fight the good fight of faith and lay hold of this healing yourself. I have taught you well—you have sat under tremendous teaching for years. To whom much is given, much is required, and I am requiring you to do this." This was not cruel or unkind. He was doing what any loving parent would do—helping me, even requiring me, to grow up. Our Father does not want us to remain spiritual babies.

I began to put into practice what God had taught me. Primarily I used Mark 11:23–24: We can speak to a mountain of adversity and command it to be removed. I did this for approximately thirty days, several times daily. I would look at my hands and say, "According to the Word of God, which tells me that Jesus bore stripes for my healing and that I have authority to rebuke these warts and command them to leave me, I now command you warts to leave my hands in Jesus' name." Did it seem foolish? Of course. Many spiritual practices and guidelines seem foolish to our natural minds (1 Corinthians 2:14). But I did it anyway, and the outcome speaks for itself.

After approximately two weeks, I began to notice the warts shrinking. From that point on, they began quickly to decrease in size. Over the next two weeks—a total of four weeks of doing this—every wart was gone from my hands, and I had brand-new cuticles and fingernails. A creative miracle!

My point in sharing this story is simply to illustrate that no one has more authority to pray for you or lay hold of God's promises for you than *you*! And at times God will actually require us to use that authority, refusing to do some things for us based on another individual's prayers and faith.

NO ONE HAS MORE AUTHORITY OVER YOUR LIFE THAN YOU DO. NO ONE HAS GREATER AUTHORITY TO PRAY FOR YOU THAN YOURSELF.

Again, our authority decreases as we move outward to the next circle. Though our family members have individual authority as they relate to God, we also possess authority to pray for them. God has given me the responsibility to be a covering or protection for my wife and children and with this comes great authority to pray for them. I recall the testimony of a man in the late 1970s, illustrating the authority God has given us to pray for our children. His daughter had several dozen growths on her hands; I believe they also were warts. The Lord spoke powerfully to him one day, as he was praying, and said, "How long are you going to put up with those warts on your daughter's hands?" The gentleman was very surprised and even a little intimidated, as the Lord seemed upset with him. As he questioned, the Lord again spoke to him: "You have authority to cover and protect your daughter. You have the right to make the warts leave her hands. How long are you going to put up with them?"

The father of the young girl took this seriously and, just as I had done for myself, began daily—and several times a day—to command them to leave her hands. After many days of faithful obedience, his daughter received her healing. Hers did not happen gradually, however, as mine did. She received an instant miracle. One day, as she was hanging clothes in her closet, she hung up one garment and her hands were the same. She then reached down, grabbed another piece of clothing, and from the time she picked up the clothing until the time she reached the rod, her hands were completely transformed. Not one wart remained—beautiful skin like a baby's covered her hands. She screamed and ran to her father with the news, and the two of them rejoiced together. *We have authority to pray not only for ourselves but also for those for whom we are a covering!*

In 1985, God used my prayers to heal Ceci of an ovarian cyst. She'd had it for approximately a year and was told by a doctor that she would need surgery to remove it. He hoped to take only the cyst, but there was the possibility he would have to remove the affected ovary as well.

This doctor was a Christian, and I knew he believed in the power of prayer, so I asked if he could safely give us some time to pray for Ceci. I really believed we could get the cyst removed through the power of prayer. Since it was not malignant, he said, "Yes, I will give you two months, and if we don't get rid of it your way, we will get rid of it my way."

I sought the Lord, asking Him for the strategy I needed to lay hold of this healing for Ceci. I heard Him clearly say to me that if I spent an hour a day praying for her that she would receive this healing. I began to faithfully obey. I do not know why this was God's chosen plan nor do I care. He has His reasons.

After two weeks of prayer for her, the pain began to decrease. After four weeks the pain was completely gone and so was the cyst! This was then verified by the doctor's new tests.

Once more: As our circles expand, our influence and authority decreases. I have authority, for example, to pray for my city, but others in my city have just as much authority as I do. All of us have authority to pray for our nation, an even larger circle, but other believers in the nation have equal authority to do so. It becomes obvious that as the circles expand, our authority decreases.

Know and Believe

A third principle in connection with our level of authority in prayer is our understanding of God and His Word. Without knowledge of it we will not be aware of His provisions for us or of His ways through which they come. Hosea 4:6 says that we as God's people can be destroyed for lack of knowledge. Obviously, if we are ignorant of what is rightfully ours through Christ, we will not exercise authority to lay hold of those provisions by faith. Paul told his spiritual son Timothy to "take hold of the eternal life to which you were called" (1 Timothy 6:12). Timothy was already saved and therefore had received eternal life. Why, then, would he be told to "take hold" of it? The covenantal provisions promised to us in Christ do not automatically come to us just because we're Christians. We must learn to exercise our authority, release our faith, and *seize* these provisions—which is the literal meaning of the Greek word translated "take hold of."

This third principle also links authority to faith. Without a knowledge of God's Word we will not have faith (see Romans 10:17). To the degree we believe the Word, to that degree we will obey and act upon it with authority. After healing the lame man at the Beautiful Gate in Acts 3, Peter said, "On the basis of faith in His name, it is the name of Jesus which has strengthened this man whom you see and know; and the faith which comes through Him has given him this perfect health in the presence of you all" (v. 16). Peter made it clear that the authority releasing the power to perform this amazing miracle was through faith in Jesus' name.

OUR AUTHORITY LEVEL IS CONNECTED TO OUR FAITH LEVEL.

In Matthew 17:14–23 the disciples attempted and failed to deliver a young boy of an evil spirit. Christ delivered the boy, and when questioned by the disciples as to why they couldn't do it, He attributed it to a lack of faith on their part. They had already been given authority over demons and had delivered other individuals (see 10:1, 8), but their faith wasn't strong enough to exorcise this one. It is obvious that our authority level is connected to our faith level.

The following story, written by a doctor who worked in Central Africa, is one of the greatest examples of simple faith I have ever heard.

> One night I had worked hard to help a mother in the labor ward; but in spite of all we could do, she died, leaving us with a tiny premature baby and a crying two-year-old daughter. We would have difficulty keeping the baby alive, as we had no incu-

bator (we had no electricity to run an incubator). We also had no special feeding facilities. Although we lived on the equator, nights were often chilly with treacherous drafts. One student midwife went for the box we had for such babies and the cotton wool that the baby would be wrapped in. Another went to stoke up the fire and fill a hot water bottle. She came back shortly in distress to tell me that in filling the bottle, it had burst (rubber perishes easily in tropical climates). "And it is our last hot water bottle!" she exclaimed. As in the West it is no good crying over spilled milk, so in Central Africa it might be considered no good crying over burst water bottles. They do not grow on trees, and there are no drugstores down forest pathways. "All right," I said, "put the baby as near the fire as you safely can, and sleep between the baby and the door to keep it free from drafts. Your job is to keep the baby warm."

The following noon, as I did most days, I went to have prayers with any of the orphanage children who chose to gather with me. I gave the youngsters various suggestions of things to pray about and told them about the tiny baby. I explained our problem about keeping the baby warm enough, mentioning the hot water bottle, and that the baby could so easily die if it got chills. I also told them of the two-year-old sister, crying because her mother had died. During prayer time, one ten-year-old girl, Ruth, prayed with the usual blunt conciseness of our African children. "Please, God," she prayed, "send us a water bottle. It'll be no good tomorrow, God, as the baby will be dead, so please send it this afternoon."

While I gasped inwardly at the audacity of the prayer, she added, "And while You are about it, would You please send a dolly for the little girl so she'll know You really love her?" As often with children's prayers, I was put on the spot. Could I honestly say, "Amen." I just did not believe that God could do this. Oh, yes, I know that He can do everything, the Bible says so. But there are limits, aren't there? The only way God could answer this particular prayer would be by sending me a parcel from my homeland. I had been in Africa for almost four years at that time, and I had never, ever received a parcel from home. Anyway, if anyone did send me a parcel, who would put in a hot water bottle? I lived on the equator!

Halfway through the afternoon, while I was teaching in the nurses' training school, a message was sent that there was a car at my front door. By the time I reached home, the car had gone, but there, on the veranda, was a large twenty-two-pound parcel. I felt tears pricking my eyes. I could not open the parcel alone, so I sent for the orphanage children.

Together we pulled off the string, carefully undoing each knot. We folded the paper, taking care not to tear it unduly. Excitement was mounting. Some thirty or forty pairs of eyes were focused on the large cardboard box. From the top, I lifted out brightly colored knitted jerseys. Eyes sparkled as I gave them out. Then there were the knitted bandages for the leprosy patients, and the children looked a little bored. Then came a box of mixed raisins and sultanas—that would make a batch of buns for the weekend. Then, as I put my hand in again, I felt the . . . could it really be? I grasped it and pulled it out—yes, a brand-new rubber hot water bottle. I cried. I had not asked God to send it; I had not truly believed that He could. Ruth was in the front row of the children. She rushed forward, crying out, "If God has sent the bottle, He must have sent the dolly too!"

Rummaging down to the bottom of the box, she pulled out the small, beautifully dressed dolly. Her eyes shone! She had never doubted! Looking up at me, she asked: "Can I go over with you and give this dolly to that little girl, so she'll know that Jesus really loves her?"

That parcel had been on the way for five whole months. Packed up by my former Sunday school class, whose leader had

> heard and obeyed God's prompting to send a hot water bottle, even to the equator. And one of the girls had put in a dolly for an African child—five months before, in answer to the believing prayer of a ten-year-old to bring it "that afternoon."[1]

If you're like me, your eyes are wet after reading this. Perhaps God's are too. If you will spend time reading and meditating on God's Word, your faith and authority, like this little girl's, will grow. God is waiting to be able to use you to do the impossible.

CHAPTER 14

THE DEGREES

Behold, I give you the authority. (Luke 10:19 NKJV*)*

We have been looking at the various principles that determine our level of authority in prayer. Contrary to what some believe, all Christians are not given the same amount of spiritual authority. We listed three of these principles in the last chapter and will now discuss numbers four through seven.

NEAR TO HIS HEART

The fourth principle that will determine our authority level is our connection to and identification with God's heart. This is often overlooked. God gives authority to those who think the way He thinks and want what He wants. When He began mantling me for my calling to America in 2000, first He allowed me to feel His heart for America. I had numerous experiences, one of them very profound, when I wept for hours over this nation's condition. The Lord was allowing me to feel what He felt and identify with it at an acute level. This gives Him the ability to trust a person. If He knows we will do what He wants, and not our own thing, He can trust us with more responsibility and greater authority.

Jesus said in John 8:29 (NKJV), "He who sent Me is with Me. The Father has not left Me alone, for I always do those things that please Him." Jesus always endeavored to find out what the Father wanted and then to fulfill His pleasure. We must do the same.

Before Nehemiah was given authority to rebuild the walls of Jerusalem, he first went through four months of grieving over the city's condition. We are told that he "sat down and wept and mourned for many days ... fasting and praying" (Nehemiah 1:4 NKJV) to God on Jerusalem's behalf. The prerequisite to the Lord's conferring upon him the authority to change the situation was his allowing God to impart to him His heart for Jerusalem. Afterward, Nehemiah was given not only the assignment but also great favor and provision from the Persian king, Artaxerxes. *Favor, provision, and authority follow the receiving of God's heart.*

This has proven true in my life time and time again. In *Intercessory Prayer,*[1] I tell of praying for a young girl who had already been in a coma for a year and a half. I prayed for a year, spending one to two hours a week in her room interceding over her. After this year—making it two and a half years in the coma—God gave her an amazing miracle. To the absolute amazement of the medical community, she was completely restored.

Why did this require a year of prayer on my part? Perhaps to allow God to work in my heart, just as He did with Nehemiah. I cannot tell you how much my heart was impacted over the course of that year. God was allowed to share with me His heart for suffering people. I was deeply "moved with compassion," just as Christ was over the sick and hurting during His earthly ministry. There came a point when He could trust me with this miracle—with not prostituting it for gain or self-promotion—and when this time came He released the necessary authority for me to make the decree. The authority we walk in is most definitely connected to possessing God's heart.

Hear and Understand

The fifth principle determining our level of authority is our ability to listen to God and discern His will. Delegated authority has everything to do with representation. We receive authority from the one we represent. Obviously, we must know what he/she expects or desires of us. "This is the confidence which we have before Him, that if we ask anything *according to His will*, He hears us. And if we know that He hears us in whatever we ask, we know that we have the requests which we have asked from Him" (1 John 5:14–15, emphasis added).

Jesus often mentioned that He was always and only doing the Father's will, His inference clearly being that this was what gave Him the ability to act with such authority (see John 4:34; 5:30–32; 6:38). Likewise, as His representatives, we derive our authority from carrying out His will and desires.

A story in Acts 16 from the life of the apostle Paul illustrates this. He was attempting to travel to Asia in order to preach the gospel there but was informed by the Lord that this was not His will. He then attempted to go into Bythinia with the same results. The Holy Spirit then made clear to Paul, through a dream, that He wanted him to go to the region of Macedonia.

In obedience, Paul traveled to Philippi, where tremendous ministry took place. He moved in great authority over a spirit of divination and cast it out of a person. This created a great controversy, and after being thrown in jail, Paul and Silas's worship brought about an earthquake that freed them. The jailer was born again, as was his family, and eventually the magistrates in Philippi humbled themselves before Paul, seeking his forgiveness.

The level of authority Paul operated in at Philippi was remarkable. He was able to do so because he discerned God's will and was where

God wanted him to be, doing what He wanted him to do. Had he failed to discern God's will and gone to the other locations, we have every reason to believe he would not have been able to operate in the same level of authority. Our ability to discern God's will and operate therein really does have a major bearing on our level of authority.

The Impact of Choices

A sixth principle regarding our level of authority in prayer is the decisions of others. When I am praying about the situations of other individuals, their actions can determine the authority level I possess to accomplish a breakthrough. For example, sin in that person's life or an unresolved issue between him and God may affect how much authority I have to lay hold of a biblical promise for him.

Others' actions can even at times affect an answer to prayer for us personally. Second Samuel 21 tells of King David and national Israel undergoing judgment. When David sought the Lord as to why this was happening, he was told it was because of the sins of his predecessor, Saul. This sin had to be repented of and atoned for in order for the judgment to be stopped. Though David had great authority with God where Israel was concerned, he did not have the authority to accomplish a breakthrough for them until Saul's sin had been dealt with.

Another example of this can be seen in the life of Moses. In Numbers 14, Moses interceded for Israel after they had sinned against God, and the Lord essentially responded, "I have pardoned them according to your request, Moses." In that situation, God forgave them because of Moses' intercession. But on another occasion (Exodus 32:32–35 AMP), when Moses asked God to forgive Israel, God said He would not do it:

> Yet now, if You will forgive their sin—and if not, blot me, I pray You, out of Your book which You have written! But the Lord said to Moses, Whoever has sinned against Me, I will blot him

> [not you] out of My book. But now go, lead the people to the place of which I have told you. Behold, My Angel shall go before you. Nevertheless, in the day when I punish I will visit their sin upon them! And the Lord sent a plague upon the people, because they made the calf which Aaron fashioned for them.

Awesomely strong words. Whereas before God had told Moses He would forgive the people just because he had asked Him to, this time God basically said, "I am not going to do it, and I don't want to hear any more about it." There are times when the sins or actions of others limit the authority God is willing to give us to accomplish something in prayer.

Marching Orders

The seventh and last principle determining our level of authority in prayer (or any spiritual activity, for that matter) is our assignment. This is the authority that comes from *representation.* Though we all have the same level of authority when it comes to accessing our heavenly Father and petitioning Him for our personal needs in Christ's name, we do not walk in the same level of authority when it comes to fulfilling spiritual assignments.

A good example is the scope of U.S. citizenship. Every U.S. citizen has the exact same constitutional rights, with the same freedoms, liberties, and protections. However, if a U.S. citizen is appointed as an ambassador to another nation, he will possess authority that the average U.S. citizen does not have. Both have the same rights as Americans, but they do not carry the same right of representation.

The same is true in the kingdom of God. Every Christian is a citizen with the exact same rights and privileges through Christ, as far as personal life is concerned. Every Christian does not, however, possess the same right of representation. When God gives an assignment, just as with any government, He delegates the necessary authority to fulfill that assignment.

There are numerous scriptural examples of this. Paul speaks of it in 2 Corinthians 10, regarding his authority to engage in spiritual warfare over their church:

> The weapons of our warfare are not of the flesh, but divinely powerful for the destruction of fortresses. We are destroying speculations and every lofty thing raised up against the knowledge of God, and we are taking every thought captive to the obedience of Christ. (vv. 4–5)

Though we often quote this in the context of doing so for ourselves, which I do believe is valid, Paul spoke here of doing it for others. He was saying, "I have authority to war over you and tear down strongholds in your mind that are holding you captive." In verse 6, he makes the bold statement that he was actually ready to punish any disobedience when he arrived. Paul was confident that he possessed much spiritual authority in Corinth.

WHEN GOD GIVES AN ASSIGNMENT, JUST AS WITH ANY GOVERNMENT, HE DELEGATES THE NECESSARY AUTHORITY TO FULFILL THAT ASSIGNMENT.

He later referred to the parameters of this authority, speaking of the measure of authority that had been given him (see 10:13–18). The word he used for *measure* is *metron*, which means a limited portion, or, as translated here, a measure. (We derive our English word *meter* from this term.) He then spoke of his "sphere" of authority. This term, *kannon*, means a sphere of rule, a boundary, a sphere of activity. Paul acknowledged he did not possess the same authority elsewhere as he did at Corinth. Because of his assignment God had measured to him a higher portion of rule in Corinth.

Acts 15 also illustrates this principle. The early church was trying to solve a doctrinal dilemma relating to new Christians from the Gentile community. Even though many Jews had become Christians, at this point in time they were still under the assumption that they needed to carry out many traditions of the Jewish faith. When the Gentiles began receiving Christ, the obvious question was "Do we make them fulfill these Judaistic rites?"

After much discussion, James stood and basically said, "I have heard all of the reports and arguments; here is what we are going to do." He then made his declaration, and there was no further discussion. It is clear that each member present did not have the same level of authority—they did not have the same assignment. James had obviously been assigned by God to be the lead person in the Jerusalem church.

No one would argue with me that I have the highest level of authority in the congregation for which I am responsible. While this involves governmental authority to make decisions and implement policies, I am certain it is also true in the area of prayer. I have great authority to pray for and decree over my congregation. I do not possess more authority than the members when it comes to the right to approach the Father in prayer, but I do when it involves the congregation as a whole.

There is still another fascinating example of this in Exodus 32. Moses had been on the mountain receiving God's law for Israel, when God told him to return to the people because they were engaged in sin. This is where the Israelites fashioned a golden calf to worship as an idol. Look at the Lord's words concerning why this happened:

"Moses saw that the people were out of control—for *Aaron had let them get out of control* to be a derision among their enemies" (v. 25).

This is a profound indication of how literal is the authority God gives to us for our assignment. The direct insinuation is that Aaron possessed the authority, had he chosen to exercise it, to stop this idolatry regardless of how many Israelites wanted to participate in it. If he had declared that Israel was not going to do this, God would have backed up his authority and somehow stopped it. We absolutely do have the authority to fulfill the assignment God gives us.

This has become obvious in my life. I have come to realize that God has given me a level of authority in America—to pray, make decrees, and perform certain activities for Him—that not all American believers possess. This is not because I know more spiritually or have more overall favor with God than others in the body of Christ. It is because of my assignment.

As I traveled around the nation with Chuck Pierce, praying for revival, there were many occasions when he would turn to me and say, "You need to decree such and such over this state." At the beginning of this time together I sometimes said to him, "Why don't you decree it?" He would usually answer something like "Because you have a great authority to decree over the nation."

I was a little confused at first, wondering about this, but I gradually came to realize and believe it was true. God has assigned certain responsibilities to me regarding America. It is a part of my assignment and therefore a part of my equipping, mantling, and authorization. Now when God sends me to make declarations over D.C. or other parts of the country, I no longer question whether I have the right. I often seek counsel in order to ensure that I am truly hearing from God, but once I have ascertained that I am, I go and obey.

There is, of course, a reciprocal level of humility that must accompany our confidence. No matter how much authority any of us possesses spiritually, we must always remember that it is delegated to us through Christ.

> Alex Haley, author of *Roots*, has a picture in his office, showing a turtle sitting atop a fence. The picture is there to remind him of a lesson he learned long ago: "If you see a turtle on a fence post, you know he had some help."
>
> Says Alex, "Any time I start thinking, *Wow, isn't this marvelous what I've done!* I look at that picture and remember how this turtle—me—got up on that post."[2]

We're all turtles when it comes to authority. Without Christ we're helpless and easy prey for sin, Satan, and life's negative circumstances. Nor do we have the means to fulfill any spiritual assignment to overcome evil and establish life and righteousness. However, with Christ as our Head and the Holy Spirit as our Helper, we're equipped to conquer evil and see the kingdom of God established in the earth.

In Daniel 7, Daniel was allowed to look into the future and glimpse amazing events concerning the end times. One thing he saw—though he probably didn't fully understand it—was Christ coming as the Son of Man to establish His kingdom or dominion on earth. Verses 13–14 tell us:

> I kept looking in the night visions, and behold, with the clouds of heaven One like a Son of Man was coming, and He came up to the Ancient of Days and was presented before Him. And to Him was given dominion, glory and a kingdom, that all the peoples, nations, and men of every language might serve Him. His dominion is an everlasting dominion which will not pass away; and His kingdom is one which will not be destroyed.

Though Scripture promises that one day Christ will return to earth, rid it of all His enemies, and fully establish His kingdom here, there can be no doubt that this "everlasting" rule began at the cross. The effect of this kingdom rule is increasing—Jesus said His kingdom is like leaven that spreads until it overcomes all others (see Matthew 13:33)—and Isaiah said, "There will be no end to the increase of His government" (Isaiah 9:7).

The church of Christ is moving from being congregational to being congressional—moving outside the walls of our gathering places and into the halls of kingdom legislation.

We are a part of this increase. The influence of Christ's kingdom has reached exponential growth. The power of this divine, unstoppable leaven is conquering everything in its path. You are part of this. The church of Christ is moving from being congregational to being congressional—moving outside the walls of our gathering places and into the halls of kingdom legislation. We are dangerous to evil, we are unavoidable, and we are undefeatable.

You were created to be a part of God's government of the earth, and when you were born again that calling was ratified. Take the sword and the scepter and begin to govern your world. Serve notice on the powers of darkness that their chest-sitting days are over where you and yours are concerned. Beginning with your *private* world—conquer! Then in your *extended* world—overcome! And finally, in your *universal* world—rule!

To the victors belong the spoil.

EPILOGUE

The Gains

As you have no doubt deduced from many of this book's statements and stories, my heart and calling is very much to see the turning of our nation back to Christ. I live for this cause. Though the purpose of *Authority in Prayer* has been to apply its principles to our lives generally, here I want to encourage you concerning the spiritual progress we are making in America and to enlist you in the cause. Though we have far to go, we are making great gains—be encouraged!

> *There is an appointed time for everything. And there is a time for every event under heaven. . . . A time for war, and a time for peace.* (Ecclesiastes 3:1, 8)

"We are a generation called to war!" cried the young intercessor, with great passion.

I was leading a prayer meeting in D.C. for the Supreme Court. I have been part of many such gatherings of crying out to the Lord for the turning of this institution that in recent times has opposed so much that stands for life and morality.

I couldn't help but think of the young Israelite generation spoken of in Judges 3:1–2. The Lord had left enemies in Israel both to test the nation and "that the generations of the sons of Israel might be taught war, those who had not experienced it formerly." It was important to

God that the generation coming up under Joshua and Caleb would learn how to fight. In that day, it was crucial for their survival. It is for us today too, even though our war is spiritual.

Another Old Testament verse about war, Psalm 78:9, has always intrigued me: "The sons of Ephraim were archers equipped with bows, yet they turned back in the day of battle." What a sad statement—equipped with the right training and weapons, this tribe retreated from conflict.

I have often asked myself concerning my generation, "Will we be as Ephraim—called, equipped, but no-shows in the battle for the soul of America?" The answer, much like for Israel of old, will determine whether our destiny in God survives or we spiritually become another has-been nation.

Our war is *not* physical. Though Satan uses people to advance his causes, the New Testament makes clear that we are not warring against flesh and blood. Unbelievers, atheists, and those who disagree theologically are not our enemies. They are all loved by God, and He wants each of them to be saved. Our real enemies are the powers of darkness waging war against God's kingdom, trying to hinder His purposes on the earth. Make no mistake: Our war with these forces is a war for the soul of a nation and the destinies of millions of people.

The good news is that a generation of believers arising in America understands this. Certainly there are also those who do not, maintaining Jesus did all that needs to be done and relying solely on God's sovereignty to make needed gains. This breeds horrible complacency in the body of Christ. Fortunately, the rising generation knows that what God does on the earth He does through His people. They know we are called to use the spiritual weapons He has given us to extend His dominion into the earth.

I recall sitting with prayer leader Lou Engle several years ago as he was trying to "sell" the vision of The Call to a roomful of national spiritual leaders. If you're unfamiliar with them, The Call events were seven large twelve-hour gatherings of young people (initially Lou planned only one) for the purpose of praying and fasting to see America turn back to God. The first of them was in D.C., in summer 2000. Eventually, the momentum led to Call events in other cities and nations.

Many of these well-meaning leaders tried to discourage Lou from attempting the first event: "You don't have enough time." "This will cost too much money." "The kids won't come unless you have a lot of entertainment, bands, etc." It was very discouraging for Lou. After much prayer and fasting, however, he and his pastor, Che Ahn, felt that it was indeed God's will and moved forward with the vision.

The day before The Call I spoke with Lou. He was a bit nervous, wondering if perhaps there would be an embarrassingly small crowd on the Mall. Since there was no registration, he had no way of knowing. Would the youth come? When he showed up early the next morning, there were already tens of thousands gathered. Before the day was over, there were conservative estimates of 400,000 young people gathered for the sole purpose of a solemn assembly—praying, worshiping, fasting, and crying out to God for revival.

This astounded many people. But most surprising was the behavior of the young people. When the few well-known performers and speakers on the program were singing or sharing, many of the young people would disengage. When it was passionate worship or prayer, they would re-engage.

What an eye-opening revelation. It was almost as though this young generation had greater understanding than their fathers and mothers. Perhaps they understood America's desperate condition more than their leaders, and it certainly appeared that they were far more desperate.

I found myself remembering all of this as the young man in our recent D.C. prayer meeting cried out, "We are a generation called to war!" How accurate he is, and how necessary is the revelation.

Last year I was ministering in Florida, and at the end of my message I began praying with the spiritual leaders present. Many were discouraged and disillusioned. As I prayed in earnest for them, an amazing passion came over me. I found myself shouting, "We are warriors!" Something supernatural came over all of us at that moment. A great roar went up from these leaders as their hope deferred was transformed into a warrior spirit.

I want to enlist you in the war.

Judges 5:2, referring to a war led by Deborah and Barak, says, "The leaders led in Israel . . . the people volunteered, bless the Lord!" Psalm 110 also talks about God's volunteer army, in the context of the Melchizedek (king-priest) order we discussed in chapter 7. The word used for *volunteer* in these two passages is also used for *freewill offering*. That's what God is looking for—radical, spiritual warriors who are willing to become freewill, volunteer offerings to Him in this conflict over who will rule the earth.

I was a part of a conference call shortly after Sandra Day O'Connor resigned from the Supreme Court. She was called a moderate by the press but was in reality a liberal who often voted against life and morality. She voted to allow partial-birth abortion, the most appalling travesty of our day. Thousands of babies have been slaughtered because of her vote. Upon her resignation there was a great stirring in the body of Christ, just as there typically is when we have the opportunity to gain a vote for morality.

Fifty or sixty leaders from the most visible and powerful Christian organizations attempting to promote issues of life and morality in D.C.

participated in The Call. The purpose was to determine our strategy in trying to influence the next Court appointment. I listened for an hour. There was great disunity, posturing for position and control, and through the entire time nothing was said about prayer, let alone fasting.

I was terrified. I couldn't help but think about the ground we've lost in the war for America's soul over the past few decades. *Little wonder*, I thought, *that up until recently we have made such little progress.* I have regained my footing and perspective, however. Encouraging news: There really is a generation of believers in America beginning to understand our call to spiritual war through prayer. And, at last, this generation is making great gains.

A friend of mine, Ken Malone, has an intercessor in his church to whom in 2002 God gave a significant dream about great gains. Though the context was a football game, it was obviously a spiritual dream. The intercessor is a woman, and in the dream she was a running back. Her jersey number was 22. The dream started at the beginning of the second half, and the quarterback said to her, "We are going to call your number [give you the ball], and the first play of the second half is going to be a double reverse."

When she was given the ball, she began to make great gains against the opponent, which quickly became demoralized. It was obvious they could not stop her, and the game would be won by her team. While the game was taking place, the Lord himself began to quote Matthew 3 over the PA system.

What is the interpretation? As we prayed about it, we felt the Holy Spirit was saying the second half represented the second term of President Bush. He had not yet been reelected, but we felt the Lord was saying he would be and that the bigger gains for life and morality would take place in his second term. We believe that the second half, beginning with a double reverse, was God saying to us there would be a multiplied anointing to reverse the gains the enemy has made in America and bring great gains to the Lord.

The female ball carrier in the dream represents the church, the bride of Christ. God has put the ball in the hands of the *ekklesia.* I am certain that the number being called in the second half, 22, refers to Isaiah 22:22, "Then I will set the key of the house of David on his shoulder, when he opens no one will shut, when he shuts no one will open." Again, this is the verse God gave me when He called me to pray for the 2000 elections and in front of the White House in 2003. (See chapters 6 and 7.)

The fact that the Lord was declaring Matthew 3 over this contest is extremely significant. Matthew 3 begins with the ministry of John the Baptist, the forerunner who was sent to prepare the way for the Messiah. It starts with John commanding the people to repent because the kingdom of heaven is at hand. He baptizes the people as they confess their sins, confronts the religious structure of his day, and calls all who came to hear his message to repentance. Then he begins to announce Messiah's coming, declaring in verse 12, "His winnowing fork is in His hand, and He will thoroughly clear His threshing floor; and He will gather His wheat into the barn, but He will burn up the chaff with unquenchable fire." All of John's ministry was to prepare the way for Christ's first coming.

At this point, the scene changes dramatically with the announcement, "Then Jesus arrived." How promising! The remainder of the chapter brings Christ into the narration, ending with the Father saying of Him, "This is My Beloved Son, in whom I am well-pleased" (v. 17).

What a passage for the Lord to be declaring while this "football game" was taking place. The way is being prepared, and the Lord is indeed coming to America. It makes no difference to God that many rulers of this nation have decided they don't want to serve Jesus, or that the principalities and powers have determined to try to stop Him.

God has already made His decision, and the Lord is coming on the scene. The Father is saying once again, "This is My beloved Son, in whom I am well-pleased." We are in the second half, where great gains are being made, and we are preparing for another great visitation of the Lord.

Among other things, He is coming to restore justice and truth. God is all about justice; it is the very foundation of His throne (Psalm 89:14). America desperately needs this justice-restoring visitation. The words of Isaiah are descriptive of us: "We have made a covenant with death" (Isaiah 28:15); "[our] feet run to evil, and [we] hasten to shed innocent blood . . . justice is far from us . . . truth has stumbled in the street" (59:7, 9, 14).

Just as in this prophecy, though, we are not without hope. Later in Isaiah 59, the Lord declares that He is about to change the situation. He is telling America this also, and we, the church, will be His instrument. Micah 6:8 says, "He has told you, O man, what is good; and what does the Lord require of you but to do justice, to love kindness, and to walk humbly with your God?" The Hebrew word translated *do* in this verse is also the biblical word for *create.* The phrase could easily be translated "create justice." The Lord has shown us what is good—what He requires of us—and one of those things is to create justice. I say to you unequivocally that our prayers and the exercise of true biblical authority have the power to create justice in the earth. And our number is being called!

God has brought us to a strategic time in the history of our nation and of the world. As you may know, there are two New Testament Greek words for *time.* One, *kairos*, means "an appointed or opportune time." It has the concept of a window of opportunity when something must be done. The other, *chronos,* is simply a word for chronological time. Zodhiates says of *chronos* that it is "passing moments without any moral impact as to the opportunity and the accomplishments in that time."[1] Notice the phrase "without any moral impact."

That is not where we are!

We are not in a *chronos* time but a *kairos* season that will have great moral implications. We have a window of opportunity to turn this nation, and we must not miss it. Daniel 7:25 warns us that Satan tries to "make alterations in times and in law." *Times* is one of the Old Testament words for an appointed time (similar to *kairos*), and the Hebrew word translated *law* means a royal decree. It is used twenty times in Esther referring to kingly decrees.

The context of Daniel 7:25 is that the Judge of all the earth, the Ancient of Days, has ruled in favor of the saints (v. 22). But Satan, ever deceived, makes one last attempt to alter God's decree and appointed time for victory. He always tries this. For every person, every people, every nation, and in every age, Satan tries to alter God's timing and plans.

How? Obviously not by changing God's mind. He does so by seeking to affect us in such a way that we are not able, or choose not, to cooperate with God's purposes. In this Daniel passage, the demonic strategy was to "wear down the saints," (v. 25). "Wear down" (Hebrew *bela*) doesn't refer to a physical weariness but rather a mental or emotional fatigue. Satan tries to discourage us, defer our hope (Proverbs 13:12), and elicit fear, unbelief, complacency, etc., to cause us to miss God's timing and plans for us.

Lest you think that God's sovereignty alone insures against this, remember that Satan succeeded in doing so with Israel in Christ's day. Jesus said of the religious community in Jerusalem that they did not have the ability to understand their *kairos* season (see Luke 19:44). He actually said, "You did not recognize the time *[kairos]* of your visitation." Visitation is the word *episcopé*, meaning to be an overseer, watcher, or bishop, implying watchful care. The Lord was saying to

Jerusalem, though they could not discern it, "I came to bishop you, to watch over you, to care for you."

God is saying the same to Americans today. It is time—with great moral implications—for a visitation from heaven. Jesus wants to bishop our nation. He wants to heal us, cover us, and return us to "the Shepherd and Bishop of [our] souls" (1 Peter 2:25 KJV). But He must have our involvement. My good friend, pastor, and writer Eddie Lawrence gave the following prophetic word on March 12, 2004:

> The Lord says there is about to be a shift in the courts, even the Supreme Court of the United States. There will be the shifting of the voice—the voice will swing into alignment with the voice of the courts of Heaven. The heat is being turned up! Even in the hot month—the month July, there will be a signal sounded around the earth of the shift. You will hear it—all ears will hear it. Your eyes will see new faces arising pronouncing the judgments of the Lord. Rioting and righteousness will mix and mingle but righteousness will prevail. It is time for those that wear the black robes to give way to those who first wear the robes of white. In the month that usually gives no rain, you will see the rains come from the high places flooding the valleys. The princes of the government of man will war against the coming shift, but the government of God will prevail as the Saints align their prayer with the decrees of Heaven. It will be the perpetual prayer that will unleash the power to raise the shield and swing the sword that will cut the chains and bring the change.

The shift Eddie spoke of began with the resignation of Justice O'Connor, "in the hot month . . . July." The rains and floods have begun, with hurricanes Katrina and Rita. But notice that the prophecy also declares that in spite of the war over God's shift, "the government of God will prevail as the Saints align their prayer with the decrees of Heaven. Perpetual prayer . . . will unleash the power." This is now occurring—please join us as we partner with God in the turning of America.

I listened with great interest as pro-abortion groups ranted and raved after O'Connor's resignation. They were shouting and cursing as they stated their intention of stopping any pro-life nominee from being confirmed. They declared, "We will go to all fifty states to hold rallies and make our voices heard."

I couldn't help but think with satisfaction—not arrogance, smugness, and certainly not complacency—*go ahead if you want, but we've already been there.* And I wasn't just thinking about Chuck Pierce and me. I'm referring to God's prayer army that has met in every state, making our voices heard in the spiritual realm. Wherever the enemies of life go they will find a closed heaven, just as did the followers of Baal and Jezebel in 1 Kings 18.

We can and will win this war. Great gains have been and will continue to be made. God has given America a great destiny. And He has given the church stewardship of this nation that ultimately belongs to Him. Don't sit on the sidelines. Join the cause and become a history-making king-priest, a governmental, heavenly minded, volunteer soldier for King Jesus.

It is time!

Endnotes

Chapter 1

1. You can read about this incredible journey in Dutch Sheets and Chuck D. Pierce, *Releasing the Prophetic Destiny of a Nation* (Shippensburg, PA: Destiny Image, 2005).
2. *Consolidated-Webster Encyclopedic Dictionary* (Chicago: Book Production Industries, Inc., 1964), 49.
3. All scriptural emphasis (italics) mine.
4. Greek *basileuô*. Spiros Zodhiates, *Hebrew-Greek Key Word Study Bible, New American Standard Bible* (Chattanooga: AMG Publishers, 1977), 936.
5. Cited in Craig Brian Larson, *Contemporary Illustrations for Preachers, Teachers, and Writers* (Grand Rapids: Christianity Today and Baker, 1996), 183.

Chapter 2

1. Spiros Zodhiates, *Hebrew-Greek Key Word Study Bible, New American Standard Bible* (Chattanooga: AMG Publishers, 1977), 1820.
2. Many other prayer experiences of Will Ford III can be read in the book he and I coauthored: *History Makers* (Ventura, CA: Regal, 2004).

Chapter 3

1. Craig Brian Larson, *Contemporary Illustrations for Preachers, Teachers, and Writers*, 132.
2. Gloria Sanders, *www.Inspirationstories.com.*
3. Alice Gray, *More Stories for the Heart* (Sisters, OR: Multnomah, 1977), 247.
4. You can read about this in my book *God's Timing for Your Life* (Ventura, CA: Regal, 2001).
5. Edward K. Rowell, ed., *Fresh Illustrations for Preaching and Teaching: From* LEADERSHIP JOURNAL (Grand Rapids: Christianity Today and Baker, 1997), 217.

Chapter 4

1. Dutch Sheets, *Watchman Prayer* (Ventura, CA: Regal, 2000), 167–68.
2. Ibid., 167.
3. James Strong, *Strong's Exhaustive Concordance of the Bible* (Lynchberg, VA: Old Time Gospel Hour, n.d.).
4. Spiros Zodhiates, *Hebrew-Greek Key Word Study Bible, New American Standard Bible*, 1707.
5. The Hebrew word is *nathan, Strong's Exhaustive Concordance of the Bible.*
6. Hebrew *shamar*, ibid.
7. William Wilson, *Old Testament Word Studies* (Grand Rapids: Kregel, 1978), 236.
8. Spiros Zodhiates, *Hebrew-Greek Key Word Study Bible, New American Standard Bible*, 1774–75.
9. Ibid., 1745.
10. Dutch Sheets and William Ford III, *History Makers.*

Chapter 5

1. Craig Brian Larson, ed., *Illustrations for Preaching and Teaching: From* Leadership Journal (Grand Rapids: Christianity Today and Baker, 1993), 48.

Chapter 6

1. Craig Brian Larson, ed., *Illustrations for Preaching and Teaching: From* Leadership Journal, 261.
2. Ibid., 258–59.
3. Bill Johnson, *www.ibethel.org*, "Tijuana Revolution" (March 2005).
4. Spiros Zodhiates, *Hebrew-Greek Key Word Study Bible, New American Standard Bible*, 1816.
5. C. Peter Wagner, ed., *Destiny of a Nation* (Colorado Springs: Wagner, 2001) 80–83.

Chapter 7

1. Robert J. Morgan, *Real Stories for the Soul* (Nashville: Thomas Nelson, 2000), 215–16.
2. Spiros Zodhiates, *Hebrew-Greek Key Word Study Bible, New American Standard Bible*, 1811.
3. Dick Eastman, *The Jericho Hour* (Altamonte Springs, FL: Creation House, 1994), 124.

Chapter 8

1. Dutch Sheets and Chuck Pierce, *Releasing the Prophetic Destiny of a Nation*, 91.
2. These words and strategies can be found in *Releasing the Prophetic Destiny of a Nation.*
3. Ibid., 91.
4. Spiros Zodhiates, *Hebrew-Greek Key Word Study Bible, New American Standard Bible*, 1719.

5. Chuck Pierce with John Dickson, *The Worship Warrior* (Ventura, CA: Regal, 2002), 108–110.
6. *Strong's Exhaustive Concordance of the Bible*, 6965.
7. R. Laird Harris, Gleason L. Archer, Jr., and Bruce K. Waltke, *Theological Wordbook of the Old Testament* (Chicago: Moody, 1980), 793.

Chapter 9

1. Jay left the reservation's spiritual leaders with specific instructions on how to maintain this breakthrough. They complied and, as he said, had no suicides for almost three years. Then they stopped doing as he instructed and the suicides resumed, with three over the past year. He is working with the leaders again to curb this before it gains new momentum. The leaders have begun to take responsibility again, as also have the people. Parents, grandparents, and the young people themselves are being raised up as watchmen to stand guard for one another. If they continue to do their part, I have no doubt that this victory will be sustained.
2. *U.S. News & World Report*, USNews.com, "High-Stakes Players," Liz Halloran (7/25/05).

Chapter 10

1. Dutch Sheets and Chuck Pierce, *Releasing the Prophetic Destiny of a Nation*, 75–76.
2. Bill Johnson, *The Supernatural Power of a Transformed Mind* (Shippensburg, PA: Destiny Image, 2005), 35–36.
3. Op. cit., 76–77.

Chapter 11

1. Spiros Zodhiates, *Hebrew-Greek Key Word Study Bible, New American Standard Bible*, 1804.
2. Ibid.
3. Bill Johnson, *The Supernatural Power of a Transformed Mind*, 33–34.

Chapter 13

1. *www.holytrinitynewrochelle.org*, 2005.

Chapter 14

1. Dutch Sheets, *Intercessory Prayer* (Ventura, CA: Regal, 1996), 15–18.
2. Craig Brian Larson, ed., *Illustrations for Preaching and Teaching: From* LEADERSHIP JOURNAL, 117.

Epilogue

1. Spiros Zodhiates, *Hebrew-Greek Key Word Study Bible, New American Standard Bible*, 1888.

BOOKS BY DUTCH SHEETS

FROM BETHANY HOUSE PUBLISHERS

Authority in Prayer

Roll Away Your Stone

MORE FROM

Dutch Sheets

Millions of Christians across the globe are constantly battling the sin in their lives—and losing. But in his new book, *Roll Away Your Stone*, Dutch Sheets offers hope through powerful and life-changing biblical truths about who you are in Christ and how to become the person God made you to be—a conqueror.

More than a book about identity in Christ, this an action plan to conquer the lies that keep Christians defeated and to see themselves as they are in God's eyes. In *Roll Away Your Stone*, readers are given sound, easy-to-use tools for understanding God, His provisions, and the principles He has established that enable them to be set free and walk in His way.

***Roll Away Your Stone* by Dutch Sheets**